# JE

# The Journal of HigherEducation

LEONARD L. BAIRD, *Editor*


*Editorial Board*

JAMES FAIRWEATHER, *Chairperson,*
*Michigan State University*

ESTELA BENSIMON, *University of Southern California*

SYLVIA HURTADO, *University of Michigan*

GARY R. PIKE, *University of Missouri-Columbia*

SHEILA A. SLAUGHTER, *University of Arizona*

FRANCES STAGE, *New York University*

CAROLINE S. TURNER, *University of Minnesota*

AMI ZUSMAN, *University of California*

DONNA BROWDER EVANS, *Dean, College of Education*
*The Ohio State University, ex officio*

EDWARD J. RAY, *Executive Vice President*
*and Provost, The Ohio State University, ex officio*

YOLANDA MOSES, *President, American Association*
*for Higher Education, ex officio*

LEONARD L. BAIRD, *The Ohio State University, ex officio*

**The Journal of Higher Education** (ISSN 0022-1546) Published bimonthly by Ohio State University Press. Eavon Lee Mobley, Managing Editor; Bertina Povenmire, Production Editor; Publishing and advertising offices: Ohio State University Press, 1070 Carmack Road, Columbus, Ohio 43210-1002. Periodicals postage paid at Columbus, Ohio, and at additional mailing offices. POSTMASTER: Send address changes to: *The Journal of Higher Education,* Ohio State University Press, 1070 Carmack Road, Columbus, Ohio 43210-1002.

**The Paper used** in this publication meets the minimum requirements of American National Standard for Information Sciences—Permanence of Paper for Printed Library Materials. ANSI Z39.48-1992.

**Paper Subscription.** Libraries and other institutions, $90.00; individuals, $42.00; association members, $28.00; students, $28.00. Outside the U.S. add $7.00 postage. **Electronic Subscriptions** are available to participating libraries and institutions through OCLC's FirstSearch. Orders and remittances should be sent to Journal Subscription Manager, Ohio State University Press, 1070 Carmack Road, Columbus, OH 43210-1002. Claims on undelivered copies must be made within six months of the date of publication. Allow six weeks for address change.

**Back Issues, Reprints, Microfilms.** Please contact the publisher for availability of back issues. Reprints of individual articles, reprints of out-of-print issues, and microfilms of back volumes are available from University Microfilms International, 300 North Zeeb Road, Ann Arbor, MI 48106, 734-761-4700. On the Web at www.umi.com. Back issues from 1930 are available online to participating libraries and institutions via JSTOR. On the Web at www.jstor.org.

**Manuscripts.** Articles submitted for publication should be mailed in triplicate to Leonard L. Baird, Editor, *The Journal of Higher Education,* Ohio State University Press, 1070 Carmack Road, Columbus, OH 43210-1002. Manuscripts should meet the criteria outlined in the Instructions to Contributors. On the Web at www.ohiostatepress.org/journals/jhecontr.htm.

**Abstracts and Indexes.** *Abstracted in Academic Abstracts, Academic Librarianship, Educational Administration Abstracts, ERIC Clearinghouse on Higher Education, Higher Education Abstracts, Information Access Co., Political Science Abstracts, Psychological Abstracts, Readers Guide to Periodical Literature, Social Science Source, Social Work Research and Abstracts,* and *Society for Research into Higher Education. Indexed in Arts & Humanities Citation Index, Bibliographic Index, Book Review Index, Education Index,* and *Social Sciences Citation Index.*

**Cover:** D. Boone/Corbis

JE    September/October 2001
      Vol. 72, No. 5

# The Journal of
# Higher Education

Patrick T. Terenzini
Alberto F. Cabrera
JE  Carol L. Colbeck
Stefani A. Bjorklund
John M. Parente

# Racial and Ethnic Diversity in the Classroom

## Does It Promote Student Learning?

Since passage of the Civil Rights Act of 1964 and the Higher Education Act of 1965, America's colleges and universities have struggled to increase the racial and ethnic diversity of their students and faculty members, and "affirmative action" has become the policy-of-choice to achieve that heterogeneity. These policies, however, are now at the center of an intense national debate. The current legal foundation for affirmative action policies rests on the 1978 *Regents of the University of California v. Bakke* case, in which Justice William Powell argued that race could be considered among the factors on which admissions decisions were based. More recently, however, the U.S. Court of Appeals for the Fifth Circuit, in the 1996 *Hopwood v. State of Texas* case, found Powell's argument wanting. Court decisions turning affirmative action policies aside have been accompanied by state referenda, legislation, and related actions banning or sharply reducing race-sensitive admissions or hiring in California, Florida, Louisiana, Maine, Massachusetts, Michigan, Mississippi, New Hampshire, Rhode Island, and Puerto Rico (Healy, 1998a, 1998b, 1999).

An earlier version of this article was presented at the meeting of the Association for the Study of Higher Education, San Antonio, Texas, November 1999. The study was supported in part by a grant from the National Science Foundation (Grant No. 634066D) to the Engineering Coalition of Schools for Excellence in Education and Leadership (ECSEL). The opinions expressed here do not necessarily reflect the opinions or policies of the National Science Foundation or the ECSEL Coalition, and no official endorsement should be inferred.

*Patrick T. Terenzini is professor and senior scientist; Alberto F. Cabrera is associate professor and senior research associate; Carol L. Colbeck is assistant professor and research associate; Stefani A. Bjorklund is a graduate research assistant; and John M. Parente is a graduate research assistant. Center for the Study of Higher Education, The Pennsylvania State University.*

*The Journal of Higher Education,* Vol. 72, No. 5 (September/October 2001)
Copyright © 2001 by The Ohio State University

In response, educators and others have advanced educational arguments supporting affirmative action, claiming that a diverse student body is more educationally effective than a more homogeneous one. Harvard University President Neil Rudenstine claims that the "fundamental rationale for student diversity in higher education [is] its educational value" (Rudenstine, 1999, p. 1). Lee Bollinger, Rudenstine's counterpart at the University of Michigan, has asserted, "A classroom that does not have a significant representation from members of different races produces an impoverished discussion" (Schmidt, 1998, p. A32). These two presidents are not alone in their beliefs. A statement published by the Association of American Universities and endorsed by the presidents of 62 research universities stated: "We speak first and foremost as educators. We believe that our students benefit significantly from education that takes place within a diverse setting" ("On the Importance of diversity in University Admissions," *The New York Times*, April 24, 1997, p. A27).

Studies of the impact of diversity on student educational outcomes tend to approach the ways students encounter "diversity" in any of three ways. A small group of studies treat students' contacts with "diversity" largely as a function of the numerical or proportional racial/ethnic or gender mix of students on a campus (e.g., Chang, 1996, 1999a; Kanter, 1977; Sax, 1996). Gurin (1999) and Hurtado, Milem, Clayton-Pedersen, and Allen (1999) refer to this numerical or proportional "mix" of students as "structural diversity." Whether such diversity is a *sufficient* condition to promote student educational outcomes, however, is far from clear.

A second, considerably larger set of studies take some modicum of structural diversity as a given and operationalize students' encounters with diversity using the frequency or nature of their reported interactions with peers who are racially/ethnically different from themselves. In these studies, which might be labeled "*in situ* diversity studies," encountering diversity is viewed as part of the normal processes and functioning of campus life or of a campus's racial/ethnic and gender climate (e.g., Antonio, 1998; Astin, 1993; Cabrera, Nora, Terenzini, Pascarella, & Hagedorn, 1999; Davis, 1994; Gurin, 1999; Pascarella, Edison, Nora, Hagedorn, & Terenzini, 1996; Whitt, Edison, Pascarella, Nora, & Terenzini, 1999).

A third set of studies examines institutionally structured and purposeful programmatic efforts to help students engage racial/ethnic and/or gender "diversity" in the form of both ideas and people. This category includes studies of the influences of coursework and the curriculum (e.g., Astin, 1993; Chang, 1999b; Cohen, 1994; Cohen, Bianchini, Cossey, Holthuis, Morphew, & Whitcomb, 1997; Hurtado, 1999; MacPhee, Kreutzer, & Fritz, 1994; Palmer, 1999), and participation in racial or multicultural awareness workshops (e.g., Antony, 1993; Astin, 1993; Springer, Palmer, Terenzini, Pascarella, & Nora, 1996; Vilal-pando, 1994), as well as various other forms of institutional program-ming intended to enhance the diversity of a campus or the educational consequences of engaging "diversity" in one form or another (see Musil, Garcia, Moses, & Smith, 1995; Rendon & Hope, 1996; Sedlacek, 1995). Appel, Cartwright, Smith, and Wolf (1996), Smith (1989), and Hurtado et al. (1999) provide useful reviews of this literature.

These various approaches have been used to examine the effects of di-versity on a broad array of student educational outcomes. The evidence is almost uniformly consistent in indicating that students in a racial/eth-nically or gender-diverse community, or engaged in a diversity-related activity, reap a wide array of positive educational benefits. "Diversity" in its various forms has been linked to such outcomes as higher minority student retention (e.g., Bowen & Bok, 1998; Chang, 1996, 1999a), greater cognitive development (e.g., Adams & Zhou-McGovern, 1994; Cohen, 1994; Cohen, et al., 1997; Hurtado, 1999; MacPhee et al., 1994; Sax, 1996), and positive gains on a wide-range of measures of interper-sonal and psychosocial developmental changes, including increased openness to diversity and challenge (Pascarella, et al., 1996), greater racial/cultural knowledge and understanding and commitment to social justice (Antonio, 1998; Astin, 1993; Chang, 1999b; Milem, 1994; Palmer, 1999; Springer, et al., 1996), more positive academic and social self-concepts (Astin, 1993; Chang, 1996; Sax, 1996), more complex civic-related attitudes and values, and greater involvement in civic and community-service behaviors (Astin, 1993; Milem, 1994; Hurtado, 1999). (Chang [1998] and Milem [1999] provide excellent reviews of this literature.)

As noted above, however, only a relative handful of studies (e.g., Chang, 1996, 1999a; Sax, 1996) have specifically examined whether *the racial/ethnic or gender composition* of the students on a campus, in an academic major, or in a classroom (i.e., structural diversity) has the edu-cational benefits claimed by Rudenstine, Bollinger, and others. Sax found that the proportion of women in an academic major field had no impact on students' cognitive or affective development. Chang's analy-ses reveal a good bit of the complexity of the relation between structural diversity, student interactions and experiences, and educational out-comes. He found that a campus's racial heterogeneity had an effect on learning outcomes through its influence on students' diversity-related experiences, specifically, socializing with peers from different racial/ethnic backgrounds and discussing racial/ethnic issues. Whether the degree of racial diversity of a campus or classroom has a *direct* effect on learning outcomes, however, remains an open question. The scarcity of information on the educational benefits of the structural diversity on a campus or in its classrooms is regrettable because it is the sort of evidence the courts appear to be requiring if they are to support race-sensitive admissions policies.

In addition to the shortage of information on the role of structural diversity, most studies examine diversity's influence on various dimensions of students' psychosocial development, including (but not limited to) racial/ethnic attitudes and values, academic and social self-concepts, civic behaviors, and racial/ethnic awareness and knowledge. Far fewer studies (e.g., Cohen, 1994; Cohen, et al., 1997; MacPhee et al., 1994; Slavin, 1995) explore the influence of diversity in the classroom or in other small groups on students' development of academic or intellectual knowledge and skills.

This study attempted to contribute to the knowledge base by exploring the influence of structural diversity in the classroom on students' development of academic and intellectual skills. The study put to an empirical test Bollinger's claim that racially/ethnically homogeneous classrooms produce "an impoverished" educational experience (Schmidt, 1998, p. A32). The study was designed to evaluate whether and to what extent (if any) the racial/ethnic diversity of the students in a classroom is related to student learning, specifically, to gains in students' problem-solving skills and their abilities to work in groups. In addition, this study sought to extend Chang's (1996, 1999a) work indicating that structural diversity was associated with more frequent, diversity-related experiences which, in turn, were related to educational outcomes. This study examines both the direct effect of classroom diversity on academic/intellectual outcomes and whether any effects of classroom diversity may be moderated by the extent to which active and collaborative instructional approaches are used in the course.

*Methods*

*Conceptual Underpinnings*

In this study, we assume that the development of students' course-related skills are shaped by students' precourse characteristics, the instructional practices encountered in the classroom, and the racial/ethnic diversity of the classroom. Students' precourse characteristics are assumed to be temporally prior to both classroom diversity and instructional methods in their effects on learning outcomes. Our primary focus is on the influence of varying levels of classroom diversity on students' learning outcome *above and beyond the effects of other variables that may also influence learning* (e.g., students' precourse characteristics and the pedagogical methods adopted by instructors).

### Sample and Data Collection

This study was part of an evaluation of the National Science Foundation-funded Engineering Coalition of Schools for Excellence in Education and Leadership (ECSEL). ECSEL comprises seven colleges of engineering: City College of New York, Howard University, the Massachusetts Institute of Technology, Morgan State University, Pennsylvania State University, the University of Maryland, and the University of Washington. Among other goals, ECSEL seeks to promote the use of design groups, or engineering teams, throughout the undergraduate curriculum in helping students learn to solve unstructured engineering problems. The original data collection was intended to evaluate the extent to which the active and collaborative learning activities inherent in group-based engineering design promoted student learning when compared with more traditional approaches to teaching (e.g., lecture and discussion).

The base sample consists of 1,258 engineering students enrolled at all 7 ECSEL institutions who completed the Classroom Activities and Outcomes Survey (described below). Participating courses and students were not randomly selected. The local ECSEL evaluator on each campus was asked to identify as many "ECSEL" courses (in which design was being taught using active and collaborative learning techniques) as feasible, as well as (for comparative purposes) several "non-ECSEL" courses with educational goals similar to those of the ECSEL courses. In the non-ECSEL courses, traditional lecture and discussion techniques were the primary mode of instruction.

Survey forms were administered in 49 classrooms. Of these, 29 were ECSEL classes, and 20 were non-ECSEL classes. Of the 1,258 students, 936 (74%) were enrolled in an ECSEL course while 322 (26%) were in non-ECSEL courses. Because of the nonrandom nature of the data collection, 46% of the students were enrolled at the University of Maryland, 21% at the University of Washington, and 13% at The Pennsylvania State University. The remaining 20% were distributed approximately evenly across the City College of New York, Howard University, Morgan State University, and MIT. The analyses reported here are based on the responses of 680 white students (58% of the sample) and 488 students of color. In the overall sample, 180 respondents (15.4%) were African Americans, 234 (20.0%) were Asian Americans, 64 (5.5%) were Latino/as, and 10 (0.9%) were Native Americans. Students were approximately evenly distributed across class years, with 57% in lower-division courses and 43% in upper-division courses. No significant differences in this distribution were identified between ECSEL and non-ECSEL course students. While the total database for this study contained the original 1,258 students, the $n$'s for the several analyses described below varied between 962 and 1,194 because of missing data. Because of the relatively large number of cases with missing data on some variables, it was decided to drop those cases from analyses rather than use mean replacement.

### Instrument and Variables

The data for this study come from the Classroom Activities and Outcomes Survey, a pencil-and-paper, multiple-choice questionnaire completed at the end of a course. The instrument has three sections. The first gathers information on students' personal and academic backgrounds and demographic characteristics. The second section asks about the characteristics and activities of the course in which the students were enrolled when completing the questionnaire. The final section asks students about the extent to which they believe they have made progress in various learning and skill development areas *as a result of taking that particular course.* (A copy of the Classroom Activities and Outcomes Survey is available from the first author at <ptt2@psu.edu>.)

*Control variables.* Background characteristics controlled in this study included gender (coded: 1 = male, 0 = female), race/ethnicity (coded: 1 = nonminority, 0 = minority; group $n$'s did not permit disaggregation of race/ethnicity into more discrete categories), and high school academic achievement (combined SAT scores).

*Independent variables.* The second section of The Classroom Activities and Outcomes Survey asks students to report how often during the course they or their instructor engaged in each of 26 classroom activities. Respondents use a 4-point scale, where 1 = never, 2 = occasionally, 3 = often, and 4 = very often/almost always. The items comprising this section were drawn from the research literature on effective instructional practices and activities.

A principal components factor analysis of these 26 items (with varimax rotation) produced 5 factors. This solution, accounting for 62.2% of the variance in the correlation matrix, is shown in Table 1. Three of the five factors related to specific instructional practices. Collaborative Learning consists of 7 practices that reflect the interdependence among students required by working in groups. The Instructor Interaction and Feedback factor included 5 practices that fostered frequent, supportive communication between faculty and students. The 3-item Clarity and Organization factor reflects instructors' use of clear explanations and an integrated course structure. The fourth and fifth factors contained 2 and 4 items, respectively, reflecting students' perceptions of fairness in the treatment of minorities and women in the classroom by the faculty member (the Faculty Climate scale) and by other students (the Peer Climate scale). As can be seen at the bottom of the table, the internal consistency reliabilities (Cronbach's alpha) for these scales were generally high, ranging from 0.77 to 0.89. The classroom climate measures were excluded from the set of independent variables to provide a more precise estimation of the effects of classroom diversity on learning unconfounded by students' perceptions of racial or gender dynamics in the classroom, which might, in themselves, affect learning. In affirmative action cases, moreover, the courts' interest has been specifically in the educational contributions (if any) of the racial/ethnic composition of the learning setting.

TABLE 1

Factor Structures for Classroom Practice Items

| Items | Factor Loadings | | | | |
| --- | --- | --- | --- | --- | --- |
| | Collaborative Learning | Instructor Interaction & Feedback | Clarity & Organization | Faculty Climate | Peer Climate |
| Discuss ideas with classmates | 0.822 | | | | |
| Work cooperatively with students | 0.739 | | | | |
| Opportunities to work in groups | 0.753 | | | | |
| Get feedback from classmates | 0.753 | | | | |
| Students teach & learn from one another | 0.679 | | | | |
| Interact with classmates outside of class | 0.650 | | | | |
| Require participation in class | 0.589 | | | | |
| Interact with instructor as part of the course | | 0.780 | | | |
| Interact with instructor outside of class | | 0.741 | | | |
| Instructor gives *detailed* feedback | | 0.713 | | | |
| Instructor gives *frequent* feedback | | 0.689 | | | |
| Guided student learning versus lecturing | | 0.578 | | | |
| Assignments/activities clearly explained | | | 0.767 | | |
| Assignments/presentations clearly related | | | 0.722 | | |
| Instructor makes clear expectations for activities | | | 0.677 | | |
| Instructor treats minorities the same as whites | | | | 0.913 | |
| Instructor treats women the same as men | | | | 0.901 | |
| In groups, some males treat women differently | | | | | 0.876 |
| Some male students treat women differently | | | | | 0.869 |
| Some white students treat minorities differently | | | | | 0.865 |
| In groups, some whites treat minorities differently | | | | | 0.809 |
| Internal Consistency Reliability (Alpha) | 0.88 | 0.83 | 0.77 | 0.86 | 0.89 |

Classroom diversity, the independent variable of principal interest in this study, was operationalized using a "diversity index" created by dividing the number of students who reported their racial/ethnic identity to be non-white by the total number of students in the class. Because two ECSEL institutions are Historically Black Universities, the diversity index was calculated so that classrooms with a diversity "mix" approaching 50% were considered the most diverse. Classrooms with a percentage of students of color lower than 50% (or, in the case of HBCU classrooms, greater than 50%) were considered to be less diverse. For example, a classroom in which all students were white *or* all were students of color was considered to have no diversity.

A preliminary examination indicated that the distribution of the diversity index was curvilinear (i.e., as classroom diversity increased, the nature of the effect on reported learning gains changed). In order to examine the nature and effects of this nonlinear relation more easily, the diversity index was used to develop five categories of "classroom diversity." Table 2 shows the five categories, the ranges of the classroom diversity levels within each category, and the number and percentage of students who were in classes falling within each category. For example, about 40% of the students were in courses characterized as "medium" diversity classrooms. This category contains students in predominantly white courses in which 33–38% of the total enrollment were students of color *as well as* students in predominantly minority-student courses in which 33–38% of all the students were white. The categories were formed using natural breaks in the multi-modal frequency distribution. With the exception of the "medium" diversity category, which is the largest group, respondents were distributed relatively evenly across the five categories.

*Dependent variables.* The third part of the Classroom Activities and Outcomes Survey asks students to report the progress they believe they have made in 27 areas *as a result of the course for which they were completing the survey form.* Progress is reported on a 1-to-4 scale, where

TABLE 2

Classroom Diversity Categories, Intervals, and Number and Percentage of Students in Each Group

| Categories | Classroom Diversity Intervals | Students | |
|---|---|---|---|
| | | *n* | % |
| No diversity | 0% or 100% | 142 | 11.3% |
| Low diversity | 6–19% | 184 | 14.7 |
| Medium–low diversity | 22–30 | 185 | 14.7 |
| Medium diversity | 33–38 | 500 | 39.7 |
| High diversity | 40–50 | 247 | 19.6 |
| TOTALS | | 1,258 | 100.0% |

1 = none, 2 = slight, 3 = moderate, and 4 = a great deal. These items were drawn primarily (but not exclusively) from a series of Delphi studies by Jones and her colleagues (Jones, 1994; Jones, et al., 1994) intended to develop consensus among faculty members, research specialists, academic administrators, and employers on definitions and components of "critical thinking" and "problem solving."

A principal components factor analysis (with varimax rotation) of the 27 skill development items yielded three factors: Problem-Solving Skills (12 items), Group Functioning Skills (7 items), and Occupational Awareness (4 items). This three-factor solution explained 64.6% of the total item variance and produced scales with internal consistency reliabilities ranging from 0.81 to 0.93. The composition of these factors is given in Table 3. Because of the interest in this study in students' skill development, the Occupational Awareness scale was excluded from further analyses.

TABLE 3

Factor Structures for Learning Outcome Items

| Items | Factor Loadings | | |
|---|---|---|---|
| | Group Skills | Problem-Solving Skills | Occupational Awareness |
| Developing ways to resolve conflict & reach agreement | 0.779 | | |
| Being aware of feelings of members in group | 0.841 | | |
| Listening to the ideas of others with open mind | 0.829 | | |
| Working on collaborative projects as member of a team | 0.815 | | |
| Organizing information to aid comprehension | 0.679 | | |
| Asking probing questions that clarify facts, concepts | 0.606 | | |
| Developing alternatives that combine best from previous work | 0.618 | | |
| Ability to do design | | 0.578 | |
| Solve an unstructured problem | | 0.697 | |
| Identify knowledge, resources, & people to solve problem | | 0.666 | |
| Evaluate arguments & evidence of competing alternatives | | 0.675 | |
| Apply an abstract concept or idea to a real problem | | 0.735 | |
| Divide problems into manageable components | | 0.744 | |
| Clearly describe a problem orally | | 0.679 | |
| Clearly describe a problem in writing | | 0.667 | |
| Develop several methods to solve unstructured problem | | 0.732 | |
| Identify tasks needed to solve an unstructured problem | | 0.752 | |
| Visualize what the product of a design project would look like | | 0.584 | |
| Weigh the pros/cons of possible solutions to a problem | | 0.623 | |
| Understanding what engineers do | | | 0.754 |
| Understanding language of design | | | 0.721 |
| Understanding engineering has a nontechnical side | | | 0.710 |
| Understanding of the process of design | | | 0.703 |
| Internal Consistency Reliability (Alpha) | 0.926 | 0.943 | 0.813 |

For both the Classroom Activities and Skill Development Outcome factors, scales were created by summing students' responses on a factor's component items and then dividing by the number of items the factor contains.

## Analytical Methods

Ordinary least-squares multiple regression analyses were used in a series of hierarchical analyses. First, to determine whether the diversity of the classrooms had *any* association with learning outcomes, each of the two dependent variables (self-reported gains in problem-solving and group skills) was regressed on four of the five levels of classroom diversity (students in courses with no diversity constituted the reference group). Second, reported gains in problem-solving and group skills were again regressed on classroom diversity after controlling for students' race/ethnicity, gender, and academic ability. Third, each learning outcome was regressed hierarchically on: (1) students' race/ethnicity, gender, and ability, (2) the three scales reflecting the instructional methods used in the classroom (collaborative learning, instructor interaction and feedback, and course clarity and organization), and (3) four levels of classroom diversity.

Finally, the influence of classroom diversity may well be contextual, that is, conditional (or dependent) on the degree to which students interact with one another in course-related activities. For example, interpersonal contacts among students in low diversity courses may well have a different effect on learning than similar contacts in medium- or high-diversity classrooms. To evaluate the extent to which classroom diversity's effects may vary depending on the instructional methods used, a set of four cross-product interaction terms was created by cross-multiplying each of the four levels of classroom diversity (low through high) by students' scores on the Collaborative Learning scale. These interaction terms were then entered as a set into an OLS regression (one for each dependent variable) after students' precourse characteristics, instructional methods, and the four diversity levels had been entered as main effects variables.

## Results

Table 4 reports the means and standard deviations for each group's reported gains in problem-solving and group skill development, although the relations among (and magnitudes of the differences between) the group means for both outcomes are more easily seen in Figures 1 and 2.

The basic patterns of the relations between classroom diversity and re-ported learning are the same for both problem-solving and group skill development. As can be seen in both figures, and with students in "no di-versity" classrooms as the reference group, the reported gains drop to their lowest among students in "low diversity" classrooms, although those drops are not statistically significant (as indicated by the "n.s." be-tween the data points). The trend line then climbs through the mean for "low-medium" diversity classrooms, peaking among students in "medium" diversity classes, only to fall again for students in "high di-versity" courses. The magnitudes of the differences between the various diversity levels are similar and relatively small. Only the differences be-tween medium-level course means and (with one exception) all other group means are statistically significant (based on pair-wise Scheffé *post hoc* comparisons). (The exception is that for the problem-solving out-come, students in medium diversity classrooms report gains at approxi-mately the same level as do students in classrooms with no diversity.)

The results of each of the three phases of the analyses are reported in Table 5. Consistent with the analyses underlying Figures 1 and 2, the first-phase regressions (with levels of classroom diversity as the only predictors) indicate that classroom diversity is, indeed, related to stu-dents' self-reported development of both their problem-solving and group skills. While statistically significant ($p < 0.001$), however, the overall relation in both analyses is small (adjusted $R^2$s of 0.02 and 0.05 for the problem-solving and group skill models, respectively). The beta weights indicate that (relative to the reference group: students in classes with no diversity) low classroom diversity is negatively related to stu-dents' development of both problem-solving and group skills at statisti-cally significant levels. In the regression on group skills, moreover, both low and medium-low levels of classroom diversity are significantly and negatively related to reported gains. It is worth noting that in the group

TABLE 4

Means and Standard Deviations on Learning Outcomes by Level of Classroom Diversity ($n = 1,199$)

| Classroom Diversity Level | Problem-Solving Skills | | Group Skills | |
|---|---|---|---|---|
| | Mean | *SD* | Mean | *SD* |
| No diversity | 2.82 | 0.75 | 2.81 | 0.88 |
| Low diversity | 2.68 | 0.68 | 2.57 | 0.83 |
| Medium–low diversity | 2.77 | 0.63 | 2.71 | 0.81 |
| Medium diversity | 2.96 | 0.64 | 3.05 | 0.64 |
| High diversity | 2.77 | 0.67 | 2.72 | 0.83 |
| TOTALS | 2.84 | 0.67 | 2.84 | 0.78 |

**Means**

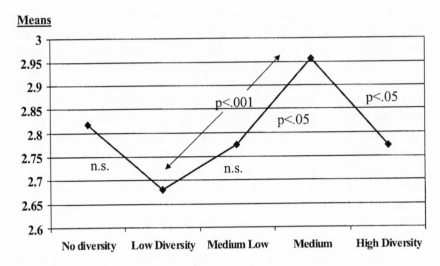

FIG. 1.  Differences in Group Means for Gains in Problem-Solving Skills

**Means**

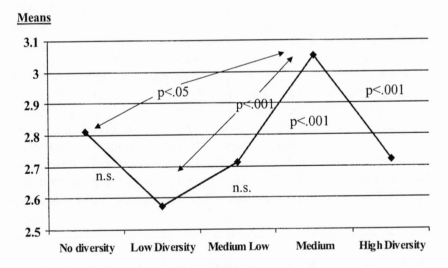

FIG. 2.  Differences in Group Means for Gains in Group Skills

skills model, the beta weights for both medium and high levels of diversity (0.07 and −0.09, respectively) approach traditional levels of statistical significance ($p < 0.17$ and $p < 0.07$, respectively), with medium diversity positively related to reported group skill learning gains, while a high level of diversity is negatively related to students' reported gains.

TABLE 5

Results of the Three Phases of Regression Analyses

| Independent Variables | Problem-Solving Skills | | Group Skills | |
|---|---|---|---|---|
| | Adj. $R^2$ | Betas | Adj. $R^2$ | Betas |
| *Classroom Diversity Only* | 0.02*** | | 0.05*** | |
| Low diversity | | −0.12** | | −0.16*** |
| Medium-low diversity | | −0.05 | | −0.09* |
| Medium diversity | | 0.04 | | 0.07 |
| High diversity | | −0.04 | | −0.09 |
| *Precourse Characteristics and Classroom Diversity* | 0.02*** | | 0.05*** | |
| Gender | | 0.03 | | −0.05 |
| Race/ethnicity | | −0.04 | | −0.00 |
| Ability (SATs) | | −0.03 | | −0.02 |
| Low diversity | | −0.13** | | −0.15*** |
| Medium-low diversity | | −0.06 | | −0.08 |
| Medium diversity | | 0.03 | | 0.09 |
| High diversity | | −0.04 | | −0.08 |
| *Precourse Characteristics, Classroom Activities, and Classroom Diversity* | 0.34*** | | 0.34*** | |
| Gender | | 0.04 | | −0.02 |
| Race/ethnicity | | −0.01 | | 0.03 |
| Ability | | −0.07* | | −0.08** |
| Collaborative learning | | 0.28*** | | 0.41*** |
| Instructor interaction | | 0.32*** | | 0.20*** |
| Clarity & organization | | 0.13*** | | 0.08** |
| Low diversity | | 0.00 | | −0.01 |
| Medium-low diversity | | −0.01 | | −0.01 |
| Medium diversity | | 0.06 | | 0.09 |
| High diversity | | 0.04 | | 0.00 |

*$p < 0.05$.    **$p < 0.01$.    ***$p < 0.001$.

In the second phase analyses (reported in the middle portion of Table 4), despite the addition of controls for students' race/ethnicity, gender, and academic ability, the association between classroom diversity and both learning outcomes persists relatively unchanged. The adjusted $R^2$s remain low and, indeed, are identical (within rounding error) to those in the first-phase models. Again, low levels of classroom diversity (relative to no diversity at all) were negatively related to gains in both problem-solving and group skills at statistically significant levels. The pattern of the signs of the beta weights also remained unchanged, suggesting that medium-low and high levels of classroom diversity may be negatively related to reported learning gains, while medium levels of diversity appear to have a positive effect on learning. None of these weights, however, reached the traditional standard of statistical significance. In the group skills model, however, the weights for medium-low, medium, and high levels of classroom diversity did approach the traditional criterion of statistical significance ($p < 0.08$, $0.11$, and $0.13$, respectively). In sum, gender, race/ethnicity, and academic ability appear to have no statistically significant effect on the learning reported by students in this study, while the evidence continues to suggest that classroom diversity may be a factor (possibly both positive and negative).

In the third phase of the analyses, with students' precourse characteristics and the three classroom activity scales included as control variables, the adjusted $R^2$ values climb substantially to 0.34 for both problem-solving and group skills. The sharp rise in the $R^2$ was predictable. Both the research literature and common sense would lead one to expect the addition of three scales reflecting what goes on in a classroom to be powerful predictors of how much students think they have learned. Indeed, one might reasonably expect these close-to-the-action predictors to eliminate what the earlier regressions have suggested is the relatively small contribution of classroom diversity to learning gains. Such expectations were largely—but not completely—borne out. As can be seen in the bottom portion of Table 4, none of the beta weights for the various levels of classroom diversity reached statistical significance. Classroom diversity, as a factor in student learning, however, did not disappear entirely. In the model predicting reported gains in problem-solving skills, the diversity index, when treated as a *continuous* variable (rather than being treated as dichotomous categories), produced a beta weight of 0.045. Although small relative to the weights of the three classroom activity scales, the diversity index weight remained statistically significant ($p < 0.05$). Similarly, in the group skills model, the beta weight for medium levels of diversity (0.09) was statistically significant at $p < 0.067$, only narrowly failing to meet the conventional $p < 0.05$ standard. Thus, these findings indicate that what happens in a classroom (e.g., the degree to which students engage in active and collaborative learning activities, their interactions with instructors and peers, and the level of clarity and organization in the classroom) are clearly more powerful influences on students' reported learning gains than is the level of the classroom's structural diversity. Nonetheless, classroom diversity, *despite* the presence of these more proximal and powerful influences, continued to have a measurable influence on student learning (albeit a small and statistically marginal one by conventional standards).

Finally, entry of the set of four diversity-by-collaborative learning scale interaction terms produced no appreciable increase in the value of $R^2$ for either the problem-solving or group skills models. Thus, the data in this study suggest that the effects of the level of classroom diversity on students' reported skill-development gains are general rather than conditional (or dependent) on the use of collaborative learning approaches in the course.

### Limitations

This study has several limitations. First, although the sample is multi-institutional and contains a broad range of engineering schools, the seven institutions that participated in the study were not randomly selected. Thus, to an unknown degree, these institutions may not be representative of the national mix of engineering schools or, indeed, of all four-year universities. Similarly, the classes and students invited to participate in the study were not randomly selected. Although local evaluators were urged to sample ECSEL and non-ECSEL courses from across their institution's college of engineering's class levels, the resulting samples may not be representative of the course or student populations (engineering or otherwise) on each campus. Moreover, the number of classes and students participating vary widely across the participating institutions. Thus, generalizations to other institutions' engineering classes and students must be made cautiously. With regard to sampling, however, the study has two distinct assets when compared to most studies of classroom effects on student learning: its multi-institutional design and its relatively large sample of both courses and students.

Second, the influences of gender and academic ability are probably underestimated in this study due to the relative homogeneity of engineering students on these campuses with respect to these variables. By and large, the participants in this study were male (73%) and academically very able (mean combined SATs of 1,241).

Third, while problem-solving and group skills are basic educational outcomes of most engineering (and general education) programs, they are certainly not the only dimensions along which future engineers (or students in general) develop academically and intellectually during their undergraduate programs. Moreover, alternative conceptualizations and operationalizations of "problem-solving" and "group" skills have been advanced, and the results of this study might have been somewhat different had other conceptualizations and/or measures of each skill been used, or if other, entirely different learning outcomes had been the foci of this study.

Fourth, the measurements of skill development in this study are based on students' self-reports rather than on more objective measures of student learning (e.g., standardized tests). Recent research suggests, however, that self-report measures of learning can be used to appraise gains in cognitive skills. Pike (1995) found self-reported measures of educational gains to be as valid as objective measures to the extent that the self-report measures reflect the content of the learning outcome under consideration. As noted earlier, the items reflecting the learning outcomes studied in this research came primarily (albeit not exclusively) from a national study of the beliefs of faculty members, researchers, administrators, and employers about what component abilities make up those skills (Jones, 1994; Jones, et al., 1994). Similarly, Anaya (1999), after examining a representative sample of students who took the Graduate Record Examinations in 1989, concluded that self-reported measures of gains in cognitive skills are valid proxies of cognitive skills as measured by the verbal and math components of the GRE. Moreover, while standardized measures have some advantages over self-reports, they also come with limitations of their own for classroom use, including availability, length, cost, and relevance to specific courses. The self-report instrument used in this study was designed specifically to gather course-level information and to be easy and inexpensive to use. One must, nonetheless, acknowledge the trade-offs being made.

Fifth, the study's design and database are cross-sectional. The concept of learning "gains" or skill "development" implies change over time. Moreover, the impact of course- (or campus-) diversity may also vary over time. A longitudinal design would provide a more rigorous test of whether classroom diversity is related to learning. It is worth noting in this regard, however, that the relations identified between classroom diversity and reported learning gains persisted in the presence of controls for selected precourse student characteristics (gender, race/ethnicity, and high-school academic achievement) and remained marginally significant even in the presence of psychometrically sound measures of classroom activities designed to promote learning. These latter measures, as one might expect, were clearly more powerful forces for student learning, but they failed to completely eradicate evidence that classroom diversity may also be involved.

Sixth, for reasons explained earlier relating to the apparent curvilinear effect of classroom diversity on reported learning gains, this study operationalized classroom diversity as four, dummy-coded levels, rather than as a single, continuous variable. Subsequent use of these dummy-coded variables in statistical interaction terms to examine whether classroom diversity might have a different effect depending on the degree of interpersonal contact among students in the course provides a relatively low-power test of the possible, conditional effects of diversity on learning. Future studies should examine more rigorously the possibility of such "contextual" effects. The structural diversity in a classroom (and elsewhere) may, indeed, have a general effect (i.e., one that is about the same, regardless of classroom activities), rather than "conditional" or "contextual" (i.e., one in which the magnitude of the effect varies depending on the setting), but for theoretical, practical, and policy reasons, that relation should be validated.

Seventh, this study examined the influence of different levels of classroom diversity only in relation to the effect of no classroom diversity at all. Some levels of diversity, independent of the kinds of pedagogies adopted, may be more or less, positively or negatively, related to learning gains. This study shed no light on these questions, and future research on the matter is strongly encouraged.

Finally, students develop their problem-solving and group skills over time and at varying rates. This study is limited by the fact that changes in these skill areas were examined after only one course. The *cumulative* changes in these areas that can be attributed to the racial/ethnic diversity in these and subsequent courses throughout students' academic programs, as well as in their out-of-class encounters with racially and ethnically diverse individuals, may be more extensive than what is reported here. Indeed, one might also hypothesize that the overall institutional climate for diversity is a more powerful force for learning than is the level of diversity in individual classrooms. Chang's (1996, 1999a) work supports this proposition, but it offers no insight into the relative influence of campus- vs. classroom-level diversity. Because this study was unable to control for campus-level diversity climate, the hypothesis that the campus climate is the dominant force remains a plausible alternative to the interpretation of the findings in this study. It is worth noting, however, that the phrasing of the survey items consistently reminded students that they were being asked to describe the activities going on in a specific course and to report learning gains associated specifically with that course. Moreover, Cabrera and Nora (1994) report findings consistent across racial/ethnic groups that students' sense of institutional alienation is shaped more powerfully by their in-class experiences than by their perceptions of the general campus climate.

*Conclusions and Implications*

Since the passage of the Civil Rights Act of 1964 and the Higher Education Act of 1965, America's colleges and universities have struggled to provide equal access to applicants of all races and ethnicities. Affirmative Action, based on racially and ethnically sensitive admissions decision making, has been the policy of choice in trying to achieve equality of access and racially and ethnically diverse student bodies.

Widely adopted as it has been, however, affirmative action has become increasingly controversial. Reliance on race-sensitive admissions received the support of the U.S. Supreme Court in the 1978 *University of California v. Bakke* decision, when Justice William Powell, writing for the majority, argued that race could be one of the factors on which admissions decisions were based. The *Bakke* decision came under fire, however, in the 1996 *Hopwood v. Texas* case when the U.S. Court of Appeals for the Fifth Circuit rejected arguments supporting the University of Texas' use of race-sensitive admissions to its law school. That ruling was subsequently extended to all admissions activities in Texas' public higher education systems, and it has shaped referenda or legislative actions in a number of other states nationwide.

In response, representatives of colleges and universities have argued that affirmative action is necessary to maintain racially and ethnically diverse student bodies and that the practice is defensible on educational, if not legal, grounds. Diverse student bodies and classrooms, the argument goes, are more educationally effective than are less- or non-diverse ones. Lee Bollinger, president of the University of Michigan, for example, has asserted, "A classroom that does not have a significant representation from members of different races produces an impoverished discussion" (Schmidt, 1998, p. A32).

A growing body of research has lent support to this argument, although the evidence is far from conclusive. A significant segment of this literature focuses on the effects of a campus's racial/ethnic climate on students' racial/ethnic attitudes or learning. These studies are generally consistent in finding that a "warmer" climate is related to students' willingness to socialize and discuss racial issues and to greater tolerance and appreciation for diverse populations. A second segment of the diversity research has examined the effectiveness of specific, programmatic initiatives (e.g., cultural awareness workshops and diversity course requirements) intended to promote greater tolerance and understanding among racially and ethnically diverse students. Like the campus climate research, this body of evidence generally supports the effectiveness of such programmatic interventions.

Few studies, however, specifically examine whether the racial/ethnic composition of a campus or classroom—the so-called "structural diversity" of these settings—has a measurable impact on student learning. This study explored precisely that question with respect to the racial/ethnic composition of individual classrooms, as well as whether the effects of structural diversity might be mediated by the kinds of instructional methods in use in the classroom. The findings of this study hardly constitute a ringing endorsement of Bollinger's claim that "a classroom that does not have a significant representation from members of different races produces an impoverished discussion" (Schmidt, 1998, p. A32). Portions of the evidence do, however, support claims about the educational benefits of racially or ethnically diverse classrooms. Level of classroom diversity was related at small—but statistically significant—levels to students' reported gains in both their problem-solving and their group skills. Moreover, those relations persisted even in the presence of controls for students' race/ethnicity, gender, and academic ability. In the most rigorous tests applied in this study, both students' precourse characteristics (including ability) and three scales reflecting the instructional practices in use in the course were controlled, the level of classroom diversity *continued* to show a positive, if small, statistically marginal relation to reported learning gains. In a regression on students' reported gains in problem-solving skills, a continuous measure of classroom diversity had a small, but statistically significant, positive effect (beta = 0.045, $p < 0.05$). In a similar regression on students' reported gains in their group skills, being in a "medium diversity" classroom was positively related to reported gains net of other student characteristics, instructional methods, and other levels of classroom diversity. This effect failed, but only narrowly ($p < 0.07$), to meet the conventional standard for statistical significance. These findings indicate quite clearly that what happens in a course is far-and-away a more powerful predictor of learning outcomes than is the level of classroom diversity. Nonetheless, the persistence of diversity's influence *despite* the presence of more powerful predictors is, we believe, substantively noteworthy and relevant to the policy question this study seeks to illuminate.

The evidence also suggests that the relation between the racial/ethnic composition of a classroom and students' learning gains may not be a simple, linear one. The evidence quite consistently indicates that "medium" levels of classroom diversity (i.e., approximately in the 30–40% range) are positively, if not always significantly, related to students' reports of learning gains. At the most rudimentary level of analysis, however, the data also suggest the possibility that low or high levels of classroom diversity *may* be negatively related to learning gains. Analyses examining the effects of only classroom diversity level, or of diversity level while controlling for students' race/ethnicity, gender, and ability, produced some marginal evidence of statistically significant but negative effects among students in classrooms with low or high levels of diversity (compared to no diversity at all). These negative relations, however, were not supported when measures of the instructional practices in use in these classrooms entered the analyses. Entry of a set of interaction terms (reflecting whether the effects of various levels of diversity varied depending on the extent to which collaborative learning activities were used in the classroom) produced no appreciable increase in the value of the $R^2$ for either model. This finding suggests that any effects of structural diversity appear to be general and not conditional on the instructional methods in use in the classroom. That conclusion, however, warrants further validation. Similarly, future research should examine more precisely than was possible here the levels at which classroom diversity becomes a salient positive or negative force in shaping students' learning.

At best, the findings in this study suggest a small, if statistically significant, link between the level of racial/ethnic diversity in a classroom and students' reports of increases in their problem-solving and group skills. The relatively consistent and positive salience of medium levels of classroom diversity is the most supportive evidence for arguments that classroom diversity has positive, educational effects on student learning. That evidence, however, is far from conclusive.

The findings of this study are all the more suggestive when one considers that the relation between diversity and student learning is at least modestly detectable *in individual classrooms*. One might reasonably speculate that, if the beneficial effects of racial/ethnic diversity are apparent in *individual* classrooms, then those effects may well be substantially magnified in the aggregate, when accumulated across the courses students take and across their out-of-class experiences in racially/ethnically diverse settings.

Should subsequent studies of the effects of the racial/ethnic composition of classrooms and other campus settings bear out the relations suggested in this research, then much of the current cloudiness in the legal and policy worlds concerning the educational effectiveness of diverse settings may be clarified. Arguments for affirmative action and race-sensitive admissions that assert the educational effectiveness of such policies will rest on substantially firmer empirical ground, and campus, state, and federal policies permitting or encouraging race/ethnicity-sensitive admissions will also rest on firmer empirical ground

## References

Adams, M., & Zhou-McGovern, Y. (1994, April). *The sociomoral development of undergraduates in a "social diversity" course.* Paper presented at the meeting of the American Educational Research Association, New Orleans, LA.

Anaya, G. (1999). College impact on student learning: Comparing the use of self-reported gains, standardized test scores, and college grades. *Research in Higher Education, 40,* 499–527.

Antonio, A. L. (1998). *The impact of friendship groups in a multicultural university.* Unpublished doctoral dissertation, University of California, Los Angeles.

Antony, J. (1993, November). *Can we all get along? How college impacts students' sense of promoting racial understanding.* Paper presented at the meeting of the Association for the Study of Higher Education, Pittsburgh, PA.

Appel, M., Cartwright, D., Smith, D. G., & Wolf, L. E. (1996). *The impact of diversity on students: A preliminary review of the research literature.* Washington, DC: Association of American Colleges and Universities.

Astin, A. W. (1993). *What matters in college?* Four critical years *revisited.* San Francisco: Jossey-Bass.

Bowen, W. G., & Bok, D. (1998). *The shape of the river: Long-term consequences of considering race in college and university admissions.* Princeton, NJ: Princeton University Press.

Cabrera, A. F., & Nora, A. (1994). College students' perceptions of prejudice and discrimination and their feelings of alienation: A construct validation approach. *Review of Education, Pedagogy, Cultural Studies, 16,* 387–409.

Cabrera, A. F., Nora, A., Terenzini, P. T., Pascarella, E. T., & Hagedorn, L. S. (1999). Campus racial climate and the adjustment of students to college: A comparison between white students and African-American students. *Journal of Higher Education, 70,* 134–160.

Chang, M. J. (1996). *Racial diversity in higher education: Does a racially mixed student population affect educational outcomes?* Unpublished doctoral dissertation, University of California, Los Angeles.

Chang, M. J. (1998). *An examination of conceptual and empirical linkages between diversity initiatives and student learning in higher education.* Unpublished manuscript prepared for the American Council on Education's Symposium and Working Research Meeting on Diversity and Affirmative Action, Arlington, VA, January 1999.

Chang, M. J. (1999a). Does racial diversity matter? The educational impact of a racially diverse undergraduate population. *Journal of College Student Development, 40,* 377–395.

Chang, M. J. (1999b, November). *The impact of an undergraduate diversity requirement on students' level of racial prejudice.* Paper presented at the meeting of the Association for the Study of Higher Education, San Antonio, TX.

Cohen, E. G. (1994). *Designing group work: Strategies for heterogeneous classrooms* (2nd ed.). New York: Teachers College Press.

Cohen, E. G., Bianchini, J. A., Cossey, R., Holthuis, N. C., Morphew, C. C., & Whitcomb, J. A. (1997). What did students learn? 1982–1994). In E. G. Cohen & R. A. Lotan (Eds.), *Working for equity in heterogeneous classrooms.* New York: Teachers College Press.

Davis, J. E. (1994). College in black and white: Campus environment and academic achievement of African American males. *Journal of Negro Education, 63,* 620–633.

Gurin, P. (1999). Empirical results from the analyses conducted for this litigation. From *Expert report of Patricia Gurin: Gratz, et al., v. Bollinger, et al., No. 97–75321* (E.D. Mich.), *Grutter, et al. v. Bollinger, et al.,* No. 97–75928 (E.D. Mich.). http://www.umich.edu/~urel/admissions/legal/expert/empir.html

Healy, P. (1998a, November). Advocates of more money for colleges win key gubernatorial races. *Chronicle of Higher Education,* pp. A29–A30.

Healy, P. (1998b, December). U.S. Appeals Court ruling may imperil university defenses of affirmative action. *Chronicle of Higher Education,* pp. A30–A31.

Healy, P. (1999, March). University of Massachusetts limits racial preferences, despite vow to increase minority enrollment. *Chronicle of Higher Education,* pp. A30–A31.

Hurtado, S. (1999). Linking diversity and educational purpose: How the diversity of the faculty and student body impacts the classroom environment and student development. In G. Orfield (Ed.), *Diversity challenged: Legal crisis and new evidence.* Cambridge, MA: Harvard Publishing Group.

Hurtado, S., Milem, J., Clayton-Pedersen, A., & Allen, W. (1999). *Enacting diverse learning environments: Improving the climate for racial/ethnic diversity in higher education.* (ASHE-ERIC Higher Education Report, Vol. 26, No. 8). Washington, DC: The George Washington University, Graduate School of Education and Human Development.

Jones, E. A. (1994). *Goals inventories.* University Park, PA: The Pennsylvania State University, Center for the Study of Higher Education, National Center on Postsecondary Teaching, Learning, and Assessment.

Jones, E. A., with Hoffman, S., Moore, L. M., Ratcliff, G., Tibbetts, B, & Click, B. A. (1994). *Essential skills in writing, speech and listening, and critical thinking: Perspectives of faculty, employers, and policy makers.* University Park, PA: The Pennsylvania State University, Center for the Study of Higher Education, National Center on Postsecondary Teaching, Learning, and Assessment.

Kanter, R. M. (1977). Some effects of proportions on group life: Skewed sex ratios and responses to token women. *American Journal of Sociology, 82,* 965–990.

MacPhee, D., Kreutzer, J. C., & Fritz, J. J. (1994). Infusing a diversity perspective into human development courses. *Child Development, 65,* 699–715.

Milem, J. F. (1994). College, students, and racial understanding. *Thought & Action, 9,* 51–92.

Milem, J. F. (1999). The educational benefits of diversity: Evidence from multiple sectors. In M. Chang, D. Witt, J. Jones, & K. Hakuta (Eds.), *Compelling interest: Examining the evidence on racial dynamics in higher education.* Report of the AERA Panel on Racial Dynamics in Colleges and Universities. Palo Alto, CA: Stanford University Center for Comparative Studies in Race and Ethnicity. (Prepublication copy, available at http://www.stanford.edu/~hakuta/RaceInHigherEducation.html.)

Musil, C., Garcia, M., Moses, Y., & Smith, D. (1995). *Diversity in higher education: A work in progress.* Washington, DC: Association of American Colleges and Universities.

Palmer, E. A. (1999). *An analysis of a diversity requirement: The effects of course characteristics on students' racial attitudes, gender attitudes, and self-perceived learning.* Unpublished doctoral dissertation, The Pennsylvania State University, University Park, PA.

Pascarella, E. T., Edison, M., Nora, A., Hagedorn, L. S., & Terenzini, P. T. (1996). Influences on students' openness to diversity and challenge in the first year of college. *Journal of Higher Education, 67,* 174–195.

Pike, G. R. (1995). The relationship between self-reports of college experiences and achievement test scores. *Research in Higher Education, 36,* 1–22.

Rendon, L. I., & Hope, R. (1996). *Educating a new majority.* San Francisco: Jossey-Bass.

Rudenstine, N. L. (1999). *Why a diverse student body is so important.* http://www.in-form.umd.edu/diversity_web/Profiles/divdbase/harvard /ilsc.html

Sax, L. J. (1996). The dynamics of "tokenism:" How college students are affected by the proportion of women in their major. *Research in Higher Education, 37,* 389–425.

Schmidt, P. (1998, October). University of Michigan prepared to defend admissions policy in court. *Chronicle of Higher Education,* p. A32.

Sedlacek, W. (1995). *Improving racial and ethnic diversity and campus climate at four-year independent Midwest colleges: An evaluation report of the Lilly endowment Grant Program.* College Park, MD: University of Maryland—College Park.

Slavin, R. (1995). Cooperative learning groups and intergroup relations. In J. A. Banks & C. A. McGee Banks (Eds.), *Handbook of research on multicultural education.* New York: MacMillan.

Smith, D. G. (1989). *The challenge of diversity: Involvement or alienation in the academy?* (ASHE-ERIC Higher Education Reports, No. 5). Washington, DC: George Washington University Press.

Springer, L., Palmer, B., Terenzini, P. T., Pascarella, E. T., & Nora, A. (1996). Attitudes toward campus diversity: Participation in a racial or cultural awareness workshop. *Review of Higher Education, 20,* 53–68.

Vilalpando, O. (1994, November). *Comparing effects of multiculturalism and diversity on minority and white students' satisfaction with college.* Paper presented at the meeting of the Association for the Study of Higher Education, Tucson, AZ. (ERIC Document Reproduction Service No. ED 375 721)

Whitt, E. J., Edison, M., Pascarella, E. T., Nora, A., & Terenzini, P. T. (1999). Women's perceptions of a "chilly" climate and cognitive outcomes in college: Additional evidence. *Journal of College Student Development, 40,* 163–177.

JE Douglas T. Shapiro

# Modeling Supply and Demand for Arts and Sciences Faculty

## What Ten Years of Data Tell Us About the Labor Market Projections of Bowen and Sosa

*Introduction: Labor Market Models, Data, and Critiques*

In 1989 William Bowen and Julie Sosa published *Prospects for Faculty in the Arts & Sciences*, attempting to project the balance of faculty supply and demand over a 25-year span, from 1987 through 2012. The book was the last of a number of similar reports and studies (e.g., Bowen & Schuster, 1986; Lozier & Dooris, 1987; McGuire & Price, 1989), all of which predicted, from the depths of a recession in the academic labor markets, that a rapid turnaround was in sight. Although the supply of new PhDs had far exceeded the demand for new faculty throughout the eighties, these works were intended as wake-up calls to the fact that the large numbers of faculty who had been hired during higher education's expansion in the sixties would soon retire, creating a swelling demand for new faculty that would be difficult to fill at the then current rate of PhD production. The intent was to spur action on the part of institutions and policymakers to increase the flow of students into graduate programs and rebuild the supply of faculty.

All of these works relied on "fixed-coefficient" models for calculating future supply and demand. That is, they projected current trends mathematically, without attempting to account for feedback loops or adjustment mechanisms of the marketplace. Yet, there is a range of different levels of sophistication. Whereas much of the previous work had been based upon relatively simple assumptions, Bowen and Sosa took a much

An earlier version of this article was presented at the annual meeting of the Association for the Study of Higher Education, San Antonio, November 1999.

*Douglas T Shapiro is a doctoral candidate at the Center for the Study of Higher and Postsecondary Education at the University of Michigan.*

*The Journal of Higher Education,* Vol. 72, No. 5 (September/October 2001)

more detailed approach, making *Prospects for Faculty* extremely rich in hard data. Indeed, its authors had access to levels of detail in their data that had been almost unimaginable just a few years earlier. Bowen and Schuster (1986), for example, were unapologetic in their work's aggregation of the entire national academic labor market, explaining that "the necessary data . . . [to break the totals down into components such as geographic regions, types of institutions, or academic disciplines] . . . are not available and we do not have the resources to gather them" (p. 195). In their defense, Bowen and Schuster were primarily concerned with the quality of faculty, not quantity. Bowen and Sosa, on the other hand, focusing almost entirely on quantity, were able to obtain finer data and disaggregate their figures, both for faculty and for graduate degrees, by individual academic fields and by type of institution. Although their model required them to make many assumptions about the future values of various factors and coefficients, the majority of these assumptions are carefully supported by detailed analyses of data trends.

Out of a universe of, at one count, 96 distinct scenarios that might be played out over the quarter century of their vision, Bowen and Sosa eventually narrowed their projections down to four main models that they considered most likely to occur. With only slight variation, each of those models projected significant shortages of PhDs in the academic labor market arising as early as 1992 and by 1997 at the latest, reversing an oversupply of PhDs during the years leading up to that point. Unlike their contemporaries, however, Bowen and Sosa did not attribute the projected shortages to any sudden wave of retirements, but rather to the combined effects of slight recoveries in postsecondary enrollments (after a drop in the early nineties), stagnant production of PhDs (with actual declines in the percentage of new PhDs who choose to pursue academic careers) and most importantly, a large, steady outflow of faculty from the combined life processes of career changes, retirements, and deaths.

Almost immediately after its publication, some researchers began to criticize the accuracy and reliability of the projections made in *Prospects for Faculty* (Blum, 1991; Gill, 1992), even as others rushed to proclaim the arrival of the first faculty shortages years ahead of when Bowen and Sosa had predicted they would begin (El-Khawas, 1990, 1991). It is a measure of the authority and credibility of Bowen and Sosa's work, however, that even those most critical of their methods generally balked at rejecting their conclusions. Gill (1992), for example, pointed to the unreliability of the data upon which Bowen and Sosa's projections were based and cautioned that some of their key assumptions regarding both enrollments and sources of faculty supply might be invalid, yet they went on to promote five urgent initiatives that institutional policy makers should pursue "to prepare effectively for a possible faculty shortage" (p 37).

Unfortunately, the next few years brought no attempts to test Bowen and Sosa's assumptions against the real marketplace, nor to revise or improve upon their effort. Instead, the focus of researchers turned to the economic recession and the impact of its attendant institutional retrenchments. According to Jack Schuster, coauthor of *American Professors: A National Resource Imperiled* (1986), "It's pretty simple what happened. We were blindsided by an abrupt economic downturn in 1990 and 1991. The ripple effect went everywhere and colleges and universities began to . . . curtail faculty hiring" (quoted in Brodie, 1995). Analysts chose to look no further than state budget cuts for explanations of the failure of *Prospects for Faculty's* projections. My intent is to recover the lost opportunity here, to hold these projections up to the light of actual data and to learn what we can from the discrepancies.

Although it is still premature to assess how well Bowen and Sosa's models will hold up over the full 25 years, 10 years out is a reasonable point to begin taking stock for two reasons. First, there is now a good deal of additional data available from the Department of Education's 1987 and 1993 National Surveys of Postsecondary Faculty (NSOPF), as well as from the National Research Council's ongoing annual Surveys of Earned Doctorates (SED) and Surveys of Degree Recipients (SDR). Bowen and Sosa made extensive use of the latter two data sources while the NSOPF results were not yet available to them. Thus, we now have access to a continuing series of data that calibrates well with Bowen and Sosa's sources as well as a rich new source that helps to extend our knowledge further.

Second, there has recently been a great deal of concern that, far from the projected shortages, the oversupply of PhDs is now as severe as ever, despite the current economic recovery (e.g., Brodie, 1995; Hartle & Galloway, 1996; Kelley, Pannapacker, & Wiltse, 1998; Schuster, 1995). Indeed, some observers have suggested that the continuing tight academic job market of the nineties has created yet another "lost generation" of scholars, like that of the seventies, who were raised on expectations of abundant faculty jobs only to be bitterly disappointed. The possibility that these new scholars may have been spurred on as graduate students by Bowen and Sosa's very projections raises the question of whether such efforts can do more harm than good. Thus, although it may seem unfair to begin judging a 25-year projection after the passage of only 10, when one considers that *Prospects for Faculty* was partly intended to fill a need for accurate data about the expected market for PhDs at the time that prospective graduate students would be likely to graduate, then the average time to complete a PhD, variously estimated at 6 to 8 years in the arts and sciences (Bowen & Rudenstine, 1992), becomes a very important milestone indeed.

This article will not be able to answer all of these questions. My plan is, first, to explain how Bowen and Sosa's model operates and what specific assumptions about higher education it employs, and second, to look at current data to explore how well the projections hold up against the performance of the academic labor market in this decade. Finally, I will try to analyze, where they have held up less well, what specific factors may have changed or what assumptions may have broken down to thwart them. Armed with this knowledge we can then begin to think about whether and how models like Bowen and Sosa's can be improved upon.

*The Bowen and Sosa Model*

Roughly speaking, Bowen and Sosa's faculty "universe" consisted of full-time, PhD-holding faculty teaching in arts and sciences disciplines at research, doctoral, comprehensive, and liberal arts institutions. It excluded, among others, faculty teaching at community colleges, in professional disciplines such as engineering, and all part-time and adjunct faculty. Although the group comprises only about one-sixth of all faculty in the United States today (the fraction was closer to one-fifth at the time of Bowen and Sosa's writing, excluding proprietary institutions in both cases), it still represents the "traditional core" of college and university faculty (Kirshstein, Matheson, & Jing, 1997). The main justification for this narrow scope is that Bowen and Sosa, along with much of the higher education establishment at the time, were not interested in the rest of the faculty, or rather were primarily interested in the ideal of the liberal arts professor, against which all academic careers still seem to be measured. The limitation, however, carried some distinct advantages for modeling supply and demand. The prevalence in the arts and sciences of the traditional career path, from graduate school to the tenure track to retirement, renders the labor market for these faculty, in theory, reasonably self-contained. Excluding part-timers and adjuncts (not to mention those without a PhD), reduces the complication of having to look outside this "pipeline" for sources of faculty supply. Excluding professional school faculty, who often have greater career mobility with the nonacademic world, reduces the complication of accounting for large numbers of faculty who may be more likely to leave and reenter academia. Thus, Bowen and Sosa were able to construct a labor market model with essentially just three components: two of demand and one of supply (see Fig. 1). The demand for new faculty is comprised of the need for "net new positions," or the overall growth in the size of the faculty, and the need to replace existing faculty as they "exit," either by quitting, retiring, or dying. The single component of faculty supply in the model is newly created PhDs. The predictability of the labor market by this model is ultimately dependent on the computability of these three components.

The net new position demand, for example, is assumed to be entirely determined by enrollment levels, which are projected as follows. First, the projected college-age population of the United States for the next 25 years is determined from census data. These are combined with national enrollment rates in higher education for each age group to project, assuming no change in participation rates, the overall enrollments for each year. The figures are then adjusted by the percentages of total enrollments that can be expected to be in the arts and science disciplines and in the specified types of institutions, in order to arrive at the numbers of students that the faculty will be required to teach. Finally, the expected institutional student-faculty ratios are applied to determine how many total faculty should be employed in each year. Subtracting the number of current faculty gives the number of net new positions demanded.

The replacement demand is calculated by applying known exit rates to the current population of faculty by age group. Life-expectancy tables give the percentages of faculty likely to die and retire per year at each age level. Historical data indicate the percentage expected to leave academia by choice in any given year as a function of tenure status, which is combined with the percentages of faculty with tenure in each age category to determine "quit rates" by age level. Sorting faculty into 5-year age categories for convenience, these three different percentages are applied to compute the total number of current faculty who can be expected to need replacement in any given 5-year period. Those remaining are carried into the next age category, where the cycle of calculations repeats itself for the next period. The model allows the net new positions demand to be either positive or negative, depending on whether the overall size of the faculty is growing or shrinking, while the replacement demand is assumed always to be positive and always equal to the full number of faculty exits. Thus, for example, an institution that chooses not to replace retiring faculty members is considered to have a positive replacement demand, offset by a negative net new positions demand, resulting in zero total demand, or zero actual hires.

Finally, the supply is calculated by estimating the total number of new PhDs to be awarded in any given year, then reducing this number first by the percentage of those degrees that will be awarded in the arts and sciences, second by the percentage of recipients who are U.S. residents, third by the percentage who are likely to seek jobs in academia (the "academic share"), and last by the percentage in the specified institutional sectors.

In overall structure Bowen and Sosa's model is almost identical to that pioneered by Allan Cartter (1976). It introduces significant refinements over Cartter's model, however, including a more solid grounding of the coefficients in empirical data and a relentless disaggregation of those data, such that most of the calculations are performed individually for each faculty age group, discipline, and institutional sector. Nonetheless, there are still a large number of assumptions made, and these can be viewed as falling into two types: theoretical assumptions that must be made in order to employ the model at all and numerical assumptions of the values of the coefficients within the model.

The theoretical assumptions can be further differentiated into two types: those dealing with the functioning of academic institutions as hiring and decision-making organizations, and those dealing with the functioning of academic labor markets. Among the first type, one of the main theoretical assumptions of Bowen and Sosa's model is that enrollments,

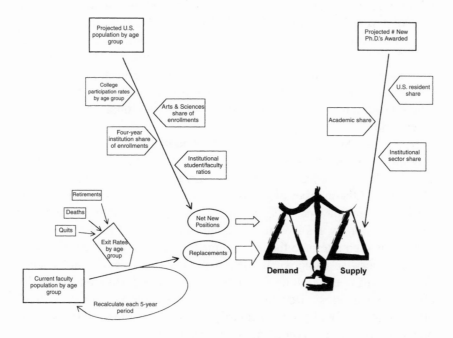

FIG. 1. Bowen and Sosa's Model

tempered by student-faculty ratios, will be the sole significant determinant of faculty size in an institution. This ignores the possibility that other demands on faculty workload, such as research and service, may change, creating other pressures on faculty size. It also ignores the impacts that organizational factors can have on the ability of institutions to respond to changes in enrollments. Tenure structures and the uncapping of mandatory retirement, for example, may reduce the ability of an institution to respond to lower enrollments, but the use of part-time or non-tenure-track appointments could also improve institutional responsiveness to higher enrollments. Hansen's (1985) studies, suggesting that changes in retirement legislation would prove mostly manageable for higher education institutions, provided some justification for Bowen and Sosa's decision to ignore the former factors. Ignoring the latter, however, may have been less warranted.

It is one thing to assume that faculty size responds primarily to enrollments. It is quite another thing, however, to assume that *full-time, PhD-holding* faculty size responds primarily to enrollments. Mortimer, Bagshaw, and Masland (1985) had found clear evidence that most colleges and universities were already showing signs of having developed alternative hiring practices, incorporating greater numbers of part-time, adjunct, and graduate student instructors into the faculty mix. They reported that they found full-time but nontenure-track positions in use at 65% of 4-year institutions as early as 1981 and that 25% of all faculty in those institutions were part-time in '81. These findings were certainly available to Bowen and Sosa, yet they continued to focus only on full-time faculty positions. In doing so, they may have been influenced by their own personal experiences with the elite, research university sector, where fewer alternatives to the tenure-track instructional labor force had taken hold.

Bowen and Sosa, to their credit, did acknowledge a number of organizational alternatives to the enrollments-drive-faculty assumption. One was the idea that academic institutions always "want" to have more faculty and that the number of positions will therefore be a function of the extent to which they can *afford* to hire. Budgets, especially in the public sector, are not always in synch with enrollments, and Bowen and Sosa noted that such alternate theories seemed to provide better explanations for the otherwise paradoxical phenomenon of growing arts and science faculties during the eighties when arts and science enrollments were declining. Nonetheless, Bowen and Sosa rejected the possible effects of other inputs on faculty size, primarily because enrollment level was the one quantity they felt confident in being able predict.

A key theoretical assumption of the second type, dealing with the functioning of academic labor markets, is that only newly awarded PhDs will make up the supply of new faculty. This ignores the possibility that a significant quantity of "backlog" PhDs, who were not able to get the faculty positions they desired during the years of very tight labor markets, might return to absorb some of the future demand. Cartter (1976) used an "inventory-attrition model" to incorporate precisely this backlog effect into his projections, estimating that excess PhDs in any given year would have a continuing impact on the market in the immediately following years, discounted by a factor of 20% per year, so that after five years of unemployment the market supply pressure of the academic hopeful is assumed to have vanished. Bowen and Sosa's decision to reject this option in constructing their model may have led them to understate the supply of PhDs. It may also have led them to miscalculate exits in the long run. Because each of the three exit rates is calibrated to age, feeding older "new entrants" from this backlog into the system would increasingly affect the determinations of quits, retirements, and deaths down the line.

There are many numerical assumptions built into each component of the model. In the first component, for example, the net new positions demand, Bowen and Sosa assumed that the percentage of high-school graduates who go on to college, indeed the percentage of each population age group who attend college, would remain constant. They also assumed that the percentage of college students who pursue arts and science programs, which according to their analysis had declined considerably during the 1970s and 80s, would follow one of three possible trajectories in the 90s: a slight recovery, a continuing decline, or a constant state. Each of these was computed as a distinct alternative throughout the analysis. There is a particular difficulty in these numbers, however, because the HEGIS/IPEDS data on which Bowen and Sosa relied do not record the number of enrollments by discipline, but only the number of degrees by discipline. Thus, Bowen and Sosa were forced to use the distribution of degrees as proxy for the distribution of enrollments. There is a significant amount of enrollment crossover among undergraduate degree earners, however. Depending on the type of institution, many may enroll in arts and sciences courses for up to half of their programs, even when their degrees are in professional areas such as business or education. Thus, Bowen and Sosa may have been led to overstate the declines in arts and science shares during the 1970s and 80s and, similarly, to miscalculate the trends in student-faculty ratios.

Finally, Bowen and Sosa assumed that the student-faculty ratios, which had decreased dramatically during the 80s, would remain constant, continue on a slight decline, or increase slightly (again, each of these possibilities was carried independently throughout the analysis). They explicitly rejected the possibility of large increases in student-faculty ratios, even in the case of increased enrollments. Because they rejected the possibility that the percentage of faculty working part-time might change, however, they calculated these ratios using only the numbers of full-time faculty. This numerical assumption seemed justified by some of the available evidence (most notably, Tuckman & Pickerill, 1988, who found no discernible trends in either direction for the use of part-time faculty), but unjustified, as noted above, by other evidence (Mortimer et al., 1985). It certainly led Bowen and Sosa to underestimate the range of possible changes in the student-faculty ratios.

In projecting the second component of the model, replacement demand, Bowen and Sosa assumed that rates of quits, retirements and deaths would remain constant within each age group and that no faculty would work past the age of seventy (all who had survived to that point were assumed to retire). Because quits are highly correlated to tenure status, however, this assumption carries with it the further assumption that the distribution of tenure within each age group would remain constant. This may have led Bowen and Sosa to further miscalculate quits if, as suggested above, new hires were increasingly made of older PhD holders: larger percentages of faculty being hired at older ages would effectively decrease the percentage of faculty with tenure in each age group, leading to an increase in quit rates for those groups as the model progressed through its 25-year span. By assuming that quit rates would be constant for each age group throughout the 25-year period, the Bowen and Sosa model had no way to capture this phenomenon.

In projecting the supply component of the model, Bowen and Sosa assumed that the number of new PhDs awarded in arts and science disciplines each year, which had declined by large percentages in the past decades, would level off at the 1987 levels. They also assumed that academic shares, the percentage of PhDs who seek academic careers, would continue to decline gradually. This factor, academic shares, is perhaps the most difficult to measure, because a graduate's status as a "seeker" of an academic position, as opposed to one in government or industry, is a subjective, not to mention fleeting, matter, often as much a reflection of how many jobs are being offered as of what the graduate hopes to get. What Bowen and Sosa used was the percentage of current PhD holders who have full-time faculty positions from SDR. That is, in order to project the number of new candidates for academic jobs, they used the existing academic share of old PhDs as a proxy for the intended academic share of new PhDs. Because the existing academic share, according to their analysis, had been steadily declining over the previous decade, this may have led them to overstate the intentions of the younger cohorts to enter academia.

From all of these assumptions, Bowen and Sosa arrived at four basic models they believed represented the most likely labor market scenarios for the next 25 years. Figure 2 illustrates these projections, showing the anticipated supply of faculty for each 5-year interval from 1987 to 2012, along with the total demand for each of the four models. In the first model, for example, institutions are expected to hire a total of 18,670 new faculty over the entire 5-year period between 1987 and 1992 (this is the sum of net new positions and replacements), while a total of 32,538 new academic share PhDs will be produced, resulting in an excess supply of 13,878 PhDs. It is worth noting that throughout the four models, the replacement component of demand far outweighs the net new positions component: averaged over the 25-year projections, net new positions account for only 3% to 14% of the total demand.

Despite the range of assumptions regarding enrollments and student-faculty ratios embedded in these models, the first two nonetheless projected remarkably similar academic labor markets: considerable excess supply of PhDs through no later than 1997, followed by a sharp increase in demand throughout the following decade. These two models assumed, respectively, declining arts and sciences shares of enrollments combined with declining student-faculty ratios, and constant arts and sciences enrollment shares combined with constant student-faculty ratios. The third model, which assumed constant enrollment shares and declining ratios, projected the same general pattern, but with higher demand throughout. Finally, the fourth model, involving the most sanguine of Bowen and Sosa's assumptions (rising enrollment shares only partially offset by increasing ratios), projected demand for PhDs beginning to outstrip supply no later than 1992. Taken together, the models make it easy to see the intended impact of *Prospects for Faculty*: no matter what initial assumptions we use, academic labor markets in the arts and sciences will remain tight for a relatively short period, then begin producing demand for new PhDs far in excess of supply for the foreseeable future.

*Current Data*

Current data allow us to test how well some of these assumptions are holding up. In all of the analyses that follow I have attempted, as much as possible, to reproduce the exact subset of the academic profession used by Bowen and Sosa.[1] This is not intended, as Bowen and Sosa also noted, to be a reflection of the relative importance of this small subset of

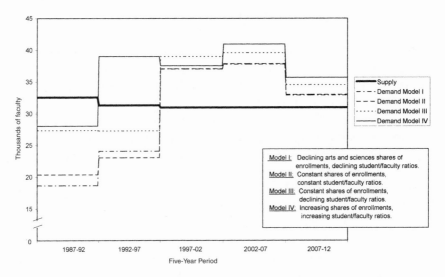

FIG. 2. Projected Total Supply and Demand for Full-time Arts and Sciences PhD Faculty

SOURCE: Bowen & Sosa (1989), Figs. 7.1–7.4.

postsecondary faculty, but rather to allow a focused look at an easily modeled segment of the market. More importantly for my purposes, it would be impossible to test Bowen and Sosa's projections without reconstructing their playing field. The danger in this approach is that today, even more so than when Bowen and Sosa were writing, the task looks increasingly like an exercise in fiddling while Rome burns. Much of the growth in faculty numbers over the past decade has been outside of the arts and sciences and, more importantly, in part-time or non-tenure-track positions and in 2-year and proprietary institutions. The continuing appeal of the traditional faculty career, however, still appears to be driving doctoral enrollments in the arts and sciences, and still appears to hold the imagination of the higher education community in its sway. For this reason it is likely that studies of Bowen and Sosa's limited faculty universe will continue, even after they have been reduced to nothing more than nostalgic lamentations of its general demise.

We know from the data, first of all, that enrollments in the arts and sciences have exceeded even the most optimistic ranges projected by Bowen and Sosa, right from the start of the decade. Figure 3 shows this trend, comparing each of the three projection scenarios (increasing shares, constant shares, and declining shares) to actual enrollments through 1995. From the 1987 baseline of 1.78 million FTEs, actual enrollments grew 22% to 2.15 million in 1995, although the highest of the three projections for that year was just 1.97 million (interpolated from the adjacent 5-year projections), an increase of less than 11%. The disparity was even greater in 1992, but appears to be diminishing if the trend of current data is extended out to 1997.

The source of this disparity is also clear. Although Bowen and Sosa projected that participation rates would remain constant and, thus, that overall enrollments in higher education would decline along with the declining national population of 18-24-year olds, the data show that participation rates increased significantly, from 57% of high-school graduates enrolling in college within twelve months of graduation in 1987, to 65% in 1996 (National Center for Education Statistics, 1998). This is shown in figure 4, which compares the projected total enrollments to the actual total enrollments. Although a major part of the growth in overall enrollments took place outside of the institutional categories of Bowen and Sosa's universe (note that the 4-year institution enrollment line in Figure 4 is not as steep as the line for all institutions), it is clear that the very first numerical assumption of *Prospects for Faculty*, the level of overall enrollments, was well off the mark in the first decade. The highest of Bowen and Sosa's three projections for arts and sciences *shares* of enrollments (the percentage of enrollments in arts and science disciplines), on the other hand, was right on the money, as illustrated in Figure 5.

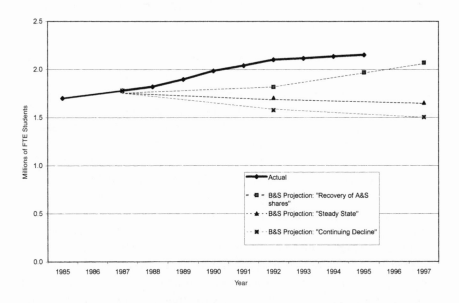

FIG. 3. Arts & Sciences FTE Enrollments in Four-Year Institutions (projections adjusted to match actual enrollments at 1987 baseline)

SOURCES: IPEDS and Bowen & Sosa (1989), Fig 4.11.

This figure shows the actual share of BAs awarded in the arts and sciences closely following Bowen and Sosa's "optimistic," or increasing shares, projection used in Model IV. Because of this, I will focus only on Model IV in the following analyses, keeping in mind that this model predicted the earliest swings in the labor market: considerable excess demand by 1992.

Despite the increase in enrollments, the number of faculty did not grow significantly over the past decade. The disparity is shown in figure 6, which compares the actual number of full-time arts and science faculty in the Bowen and Sosa universe with the numbers projected by Model IV. Faculty numbers increased by about 3% between 1987 and 1992, from 145,120 to 149,390, larger than the increase of just 0.8% projected by Model IV, but still considerably less than what the projected increase would be if we were to adjust that projection to reflect the actual enrollment growth observed above. That is, knowing that Bowen and Sosa based their projected net new positions on enrollments, if we "correct" their guess on enrollments and keep the rest of their formula intact, Model IV would have projected an increase in faculty of 12.4%, bringing the total number of full-time faculty up to 163,120 in 1992. This shows that the disparity between the projections and reality resulted from more than just the missed assumption on enrollments. In fact, it suggests that guessing correctly on enrollments would not have helped much at all to improve the accuracy of Bowen and Sosa's projections.

The difference is clearly reflected in student-faculty ratios. Bowen and Sosa were reluctant to project any increase in these ratios at all, thinking it most likely, from organizational considerations, that they would remain constant over the next 25 years, even after having dropped by over 26% in the previous decade. However, under the increasing enrollments assumption, they grudgingly allowed that it was possible for the ratios also to increase modestly, by no more than 5%. This is the figure they used in calculating the net new positions demand for Model IV, although they also allowed that the ratios could increase still further "if there were a severe financial crisis in higher education." In reality, the ratio of full-time equivalent arts and science students to full time PhD-holding arts and science faculty in 4-year institutions (the definition used by Bowen and Sosa) increased by 14.7% between 1987 and 1992, according to NSOPF and IPEDS data. In other words, although enrollments grew considerably, student-faculty ratios grew right along with them, leaving overall faculty numbers relatively flat. Thus, Bowen and Sosa's first theoretical assumption about institutional behavior, that enrollments alone would drive faculty size, completely failed to hold during the first decade of the model.

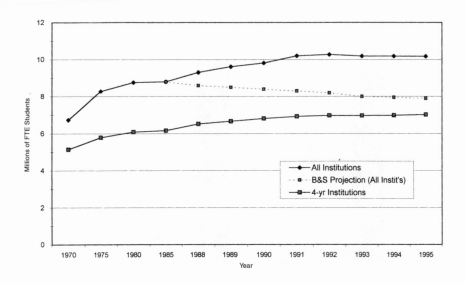

FIG. 4. Total FTE Enrollments

SOURCES: HEGIS/IPEDS and Bowen & Sosa (1989), Fig. 3.6.

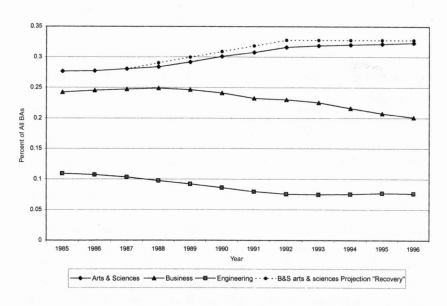

FIG. 5. Trends in Degrees Conferred: Percent of BAs at All Four-Year Institutions (projections adjusted to match actual percentages at 1985 baseline)

SOURCES: IPEDS Completion Survey and Bowen & Sosa (1989), Table 4.5.

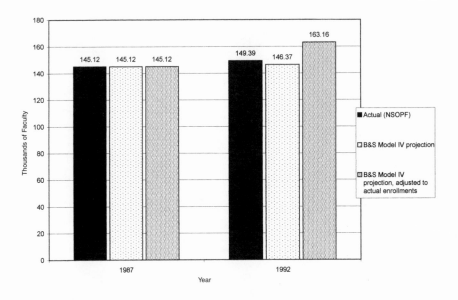

FIG. 6. Number of Full-Time Arts and Science PhD Faculty at Four-Year Institutions

SOURCES: NSOPF data, Bowen & Sosa (1989), Model IV, and author's calculations.

We turn next to the supply side of the model. Recall that all four of Bowen and Sosa's basic scenarios assumed a roughly constant production of PhDs throughout the 25-year period. The actual figures for the first decade, shown in Figure 7, are quite different. The number of doctorates awarded in arts and science disciplines grew steadily from 1987 to 1996, increasing by over 31%, from 17,460 to 22,920. The total number of PhDs awarded are only part of the picture, however. We must also estimate the percentage of these graduates who were seeking academic employment, or the academic share. For this I used the SED databases, rather than SDR, because SED has the advantage of focusing on new PhD recipients. Bowen and Sosa used the current academic share of existing PhDs as proxy for the intended academic share of new PhDs. The best proxy variable in SED, by contrast, is the percentage of new arts and science PhDs with definite employment plans in the United States who had job commitments in higher education (excluding post-docs). That is, of those doctoral recipients who had job offers at graduation, what percentage of those offers were in academia? This figure takes account of the percentage intending to stay in the United States, thus automatically correcting for the growth in the proportion of PhDs awarded to nonresidents in the past decade. Moreover, as a proxy for the academic share of job seekers this number should tend, if anything, to understate

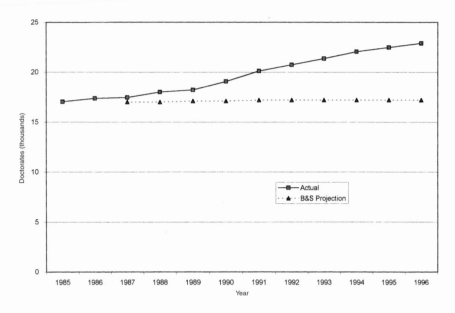

FIG. 7. Doctorates Awarded in Arts & Sciences

SOURCE: SED Doctorate Records File.

the academic share in the tight academic labor market of the past decade, as we would expect higher percentages of academic job seekers to be without offers at graduation than of nonacademic job seekers. (Recall that Bowen and Sosa's SDR proxy was more likely to have overstated the academic share of new PhDs.) The data for this quantity are shown in Figure 8, which indicates that the academic share remained roughly constant at around 50% from the mid-eighties through at least 1993, the last year for which data were available.

Applying this information to the numbers of PhDs from Figure 7 yields the top curve of Figure 9, which is the estimate of the actual number of new PhD recipients in the arts and sciences who sought faculty positions, or the observed supply of faculty. Notice the sharp increase in the slope of this curve from 1987 onward, which roughly parallels the increase in the total number of PhDs awarded (Fig. 7) reduced by the constant 50% academic share (Fig. 8). This is juxtaposed in Figure 9 with the projected faculty supply (eight thousand per year, following Bowen and Sosa's assumptions of constant PhD production and academic shares). By contrast, the lower curve of Figure 9 represents the actual number of these new PhDs hired each year (the demand), also from SED data. The gap between the number of candidates and the number of hires gives an indication of the real tightness of the academic labor mar-

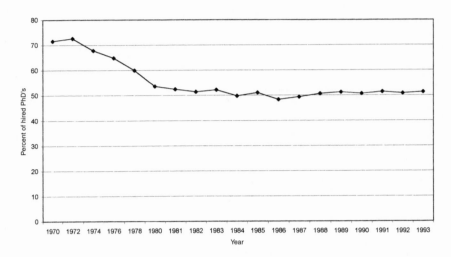

FIG. 8. Academic Share: Percent of New Arts & Science PhDs with Definite Employment Plans in the United States Whose Job Commitments Were in Higher Education

SOURCES: NCES 1995 Condition of Education, SED.

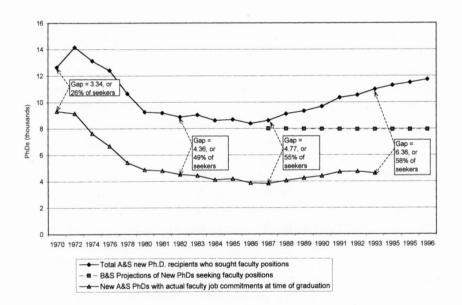

FIG. 9. Supply of New Academic PhDs in Arts & Sciences

SOURCES: SED, Bowen & Sosa (1989), Table 6.6, and author's calculations.

ket for new PhDs, increasing steadily throughout the eighties and early nineties. As indicated in the figure, these calculations suggest that 4,360 doctoral recipients, or 49% of the academic job seekers, did not find positions at the time of graduation in 1982. This gap grew to 4,770, or 55% of the candidates in 1987, and an astonishing 6,360 PhDs, or 58% of the candidates, in 1993, the last year for which data were available.

Thus, Bowen and Sosa's projections slightly underestimated the net new positions component of demand and greatly underestimated supply. What about the replacement component of demand? This quantity cannot be determined directly, because we have no data on how many faculty actually exited the profession in any given year. We turn instead to the overall balance of supply and demand, where the number of replacements can be imputed from other quantities. Table 1 compares the supply and demand data from the 5-year period 1987–1992 with the projections arising from Model IV over the same period. (Note that, up to this point, I have been using figures for all arts and science PhDs in the calculations of supply. These must now be reduced, following Bowen and Sosa's method, by the percentage expected to be hired by 4-year institutions. Thus, for example, the roughly eight thousand academic job seekers per year projected in Figure 9 becomes a total of not 40,000, but only 33,498 projected to be available for hire over the 5-year period in Table 1.) The actual net new positions number, 4,263 faculty, comes from NSOPF data (see Fig. 6), while the actual number of new PhDs hired, 21,278 faculty, comes from the sum of all new PhD job commitments in academia over the 5 years (see the lower curve of Fig. 9), multiplied by the 84% (using Bowen and Sosa's figure again) expected to go to 4-yr institutions. Finally, the "actual" number of replacements demanded, 17,015 faculty, is computed by the difference between the number of new PhDs hired and the net new positions.

The first quantity to notice in Table 1 is the huge discrepancy in excess supply, 12,866 PhDs, indicated by the difference between the actual data and the projections. This excess is not the total number of actual jobless faculty candidates during the period (18,300), but merely the total number above and beyond those who were expected to be jobless, given the projections of Model IV. This is one measure of the nineties' "crisis" in the academic labor market: the disparity between the actual number of jobless PhDs and the expected number, if one were to have believed these widely publicized projections. Interestingly, it is almost evenly split between the higher than projected number of PhDs awarded (roughly 6,100) and the lower than projected number of PhDs hired (roughly 6,800).

The second important discrepancy in Table 1 is the almost ten thousand fewer replacements actually demanded than projected. It is hard to imagine that this many fewer faculty (only 37% of the projected quantity) either quit, retired or died during this 5-year period than Bowen and Sosa's life expectancy tables and age-specific quit and retirement rates had anticipated. There simply is not that much room for error during the first 5-year period, no matter how poorly specified those coefficients are. Instead, this analysis forces us to assume that far more exits actually did take place, and that they were replaced not with new PhDs as specified in the model, but with older PhDs from the backlog of jobless candidates built up over the previous decade of excess supply. The sharp growth in postdoctoral research positions during this period (Barkume, 1996–97; Brodie, 1995) is certainly a manifestation of this phenomenon, because post-docs provide a mechanism for returning jobless PhDs into the supply pipeline after one to 3 years.

We can go further in analyzing the sources of the gap between expected net new positions and actual net new positions. First, some of the difference is made up by relaxing Bowen and Sosa's assumption of constant ratios of part-time to full-time faculty, which we know not to have held up in the nineties. Figure 10 shows that the percentage of faculty who worked part time grew from 11% in 1987 to 14% in 1992. If we convert the earlier calculations of student-faculty ratios to also take account of part-time faculty, the 14.7% increase in the ratio of FTE student enrollments to FT faculty is reduced to only a 12.6% increase when using the number of FTE faculty.[2]

TABLE 1

Supply and Demand for Arts and Science PhD Faculty in All Four-Year Institutions
(Totals for Five-Year Period from 1987 to 1992)

|  | Actual | Model IV Projections | Difference |
|---|---|---|---|
| Net new positions | 4,263 | 1,200 | 3,063 |
| Replacements | 17,015* | 26,863 | (9,848) |
| New PhDs hired (Total demand) | 21,278 | 28,063** | (6,785) |
| New PhDs earned (Supply) | 39,578 | 33,498 | 6,081 |
| Excess supply | 18,300 | 5,435 | 12,866 |
| Excess as % of supply | 46% | 16% |  |

* Imputed by subtracting net new positions from the number of new PhDs hired.
** Computed by adding projected net new positions and projected replacements (exits).

Still more insight can be gained from examining changes in the age profile of faculty from 1987 to 1992. In Figure 11 we see that the overall age distribution for full-time faculty has shifted to the right, reflecting the aging process of a substantially fixed body of continuing faculty during this period. We also see, however, that the distribution has flattened somewhat, with the large spike at the 45–49 age group in 1987 (representing the expansion hires of the sixties) shrinking relative to the neighboring groups as it moves into the 50–54 age group in 1992. This illustrates the general principle that Bowen and Sosa noted in rejecting the "mass retirements" hypothesis: that non-normal distributions will become more normal over time, as the processes of attrition (quit and death rates) and replacement whittle down the spikes.

Looking more closely, we can also see that significant numbers of new hires are taking place in the 40–44 and 45–49 age groups. This is evident because these groups in 1992 are as large as, or larger than, the preceding age group was in 1987. Thus, for example, even though we know that a certain number of the faculty who were 40–44 years old in 1987 will have quit or died by 1992 (between 8% and 16%, according to Bowen and Sosa's exit assumptions), the 45–49 age group in 1992 is no smaller at all. Thus, an equivalent number of replacement hires must

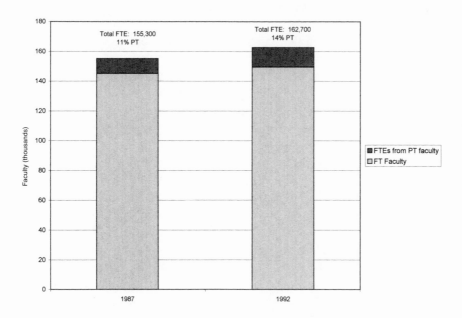

FIG. 10. FTE PhD Faculty in Arts & Sciences at Four-Year Institutions

SOURCE: NSOPF '88, '93.

have been made directly into the 45–49 age group. These hires are not likely to have been newly awarded PhDs, however, nor even new PhDs coming off of one- or 2-year post-docs: the median age at receipt of the PhD increased only slightly during this period, from 33.8 years in 1988 to 34.2 in 1993, not enough to supply a significant increase in numbers of new PhDs in the 45–49 age group (Sanderson, Dugoni, Hoffer, & Selfa, 1999). Rather, as we deduced earlier, these must be older PhD holders who were part of the "backlog" of excess supply from the previous decade.

Finally, it is also apparent from the figure that faculty are increasingly working past age 70, and even working full-time at that age, contrary to the retirement assumptions of Bowen and Sosa. Although these numbers are not large, they are clearly significant, nearly quadrupling from just 460 faculty in 1987 to 1,700 in 1992. This phenomenon appears to defy Holden and Hansen's (1989) work, which maintained that, despite the uncapping of mandatory retirement as a result of the 1986 Age Discrimination in Employment Act (ADEA) Amendments, "there is little solid evidence that faculty members wish to work beyond age 70" (p.83).

Looking now at the age distribution of part-time faculty (Fig. 12) we also see some interesting trends. First, there are striking increases in the number of part-time faculty in each of the 45–69 age ranges from 1987 to 1992. It is possible that some of these new part-timers are former full-time faculty who have chosen to switch to part-time, but the more likely explanation, at least in the 45–59 age groups, seems to be that significant numbers of new, older PhD holders who were not previously in academia have been hired to work part-time, again in agreement with the "backlog" theory. In the 60–69 age ranges, on the other hand, it is reasonable to assume that these new part-timers represent existing full-time faculty who would otherwise have retired, but chose instead to continue on part-time. This last proposition, combined with the increase in the number of over-70 full-time faculty, represents the only real evidence we have that Bowen and Sosa's model may have overestimated the replacement demand due to retirements.

The small possible reductions in retirement rates, however, even combined with the moderate increases in part-time faculty, still only make up for a small portion of the gap in actual faculty numbers as compared to the expected numbers of Model IV, given what we know about enrollment growth in the arts and sciences. Another possible partial explanation is that the use of arts and science degrees as proxy for enrollments has caused us to overestimate the true growth in arts and science shares of enrollments. Because business and engineering degrees, for example, both declined as percentages of all BAs between 1987 and 1996 (see

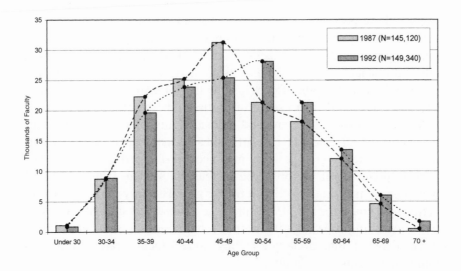

Fig. 11. Distribution of Full-Time Faculty by Age: All PhD-Holding Faculty in Arts &
Sciences at Four-Year Institutions

Source: NSOPF '88, '93.

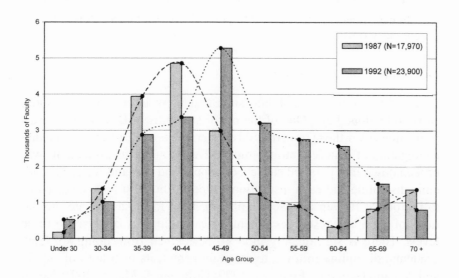

Fig. 12. Distribution of Part-Time Faculty by Age: All PhD-Holding Faculty in Arts &
Sciences at Four-Year Institutions

Source: NSOPF '88, '93.

Fig. 5), those portions of total arts and science *course* enrollments that were previously filled by students pursuing degrees in business and engineering would also have declined. In other words, an increase of one arts and science degree at the expense of, say, one business degree may really only be a net gain of perhaps one half of a student course load in arts and sciences if, as in some institutions, the business student takes half of her courses in the arts and sciences. This phenomenon, depending on the actual percentage of arts and sciences courses taken by non-arts and science degree seekers, may account for perhaps another percentage point off of the observed increase in student-faculty ratios. It would be significant, but still not fill the gap. The only remaining explanation to account for the 11% of increase in observed student-faculty ratios outstanding is perhaps the simplest: institutions ignored enrollment-driven demand, intentionally allowing student-faculty ratios to increase rather than hiring new faculty.

Summing up, the data have shown that Bowen and Sosa overestimated replacement demand for faculty during the first two 5-year periods, but also that they underestimated the growth in both undergraduate enrollments and PhDs awarded. In the end, the low level of replacement demand and high level of supply overwhelmed the balance of the labor market. The situation was exacerbated by the addition of a large "thumb" on the scale: the total demand for faculty was met partly by older PhDs and by part-time faculty, in defiance of the assumptions of Bowen and Sosa's model that limited their vision to new PhDs and full-time faculty only.

*Implications and Discussion*

As a first comment, I should state that there is clearly much more work to be done here. One of the major strengths of Bowen and Sosa's projections over those of earlier forecasters, as noted earlier, was the dis-aggregation of data fed into the model. Every one of its projections was broken down into detailed subsets of supply and demand for each academic discipline and each institutional type. Although I have taken pains to reproduce Bowen and Sosa's playing field in the aggregate, limitations of time and resources precluded extending my analysis to these levels. There is significantly more to be learned from doing so. Each academic discipline follows, to a certain extent, its own laws of supply and demand (see, e.g., Freeman, 1999; Goldman & Massy, 2001; Nerad & Cerny, 1999; Pollak, 1999). In fact, Burke's (1988) study found evidence of significant variation in the labor market for faculty among specialties within disciplines at research universities. Each institutional sector also tends to hire faculty differently, in accord with variations in educational mission, leading to what Youn (1988) calls "a multiplicity of overlapping markets." Caution is required here, however: although Fairweather (1995) finds some evidence for the segmentation of the faculty labor market by institutional sector, he warns that his data are also consistent with the idea of a single national market for faculty, undifferentiated by institutional type. Fairweather's results, therefore, based on quantitative analysis of national (NSOPF) data, force us to qualify several earlier depictions of stark differences among institutional sectors (e.g. Caplow & McGee, 1977; Clark, 1987; Finnegan, 1993). It may be that formerly distinct segments of the academic labor market have become more consolidated in recent years, as the excess supply of PhDs allowed institutions of diverse mission to demand higher, more uniform scholarly credentials of prospective faculty, at the same time that anxious job seekers were forced to forgo the luxury of being able to choose an institutional sector on the basis of mission. Finnegan observed both of these phenomena among the cohort of faculty hired during the oversupplied market for PhDs in the 1970s. As long as the jury is still out on this question, however, it certainly seems prudent to disaggregate data by institutional sector where feasible. Finally, there is also some evidence that disaggregation by geographical region, perhaps even more than by discipline or institutional sector, may further improve our ability to forecast academic labor markets (Chatman & Jung, 1992; McGinnis & Long, 1988).

My analysis has also raised some interesting questions that suggest a need for further data collection. For example, can we measure the actual number of quits, rather than imputing the number from other values, as I have done? If so, it would be possible to test independently the various quit rate assumptions of Bowen and Sosa's model and thus more completely assess its validity. Similarly, it would be helpful to be able to determine more accurately the sources of supply. How many new hires are in fact taken from the ranks of older PhDs, and what are the career histories of those individuals? So far the evidence is only secondhand, as in my analysis, or anecdotal (but see, e.g., Rosenfeld & Jones, 1988, for an older look at a single discipline).

Two other questions that did not come up in this analysis may also help to improve the model. The first has to do with the use of graduate student teaching assistants in research and doctoral universities. There appears to have been a significant increase in such usage in the past decade, which Goldman and Massy (2001) suggest might explain some of the reduction in hiring of full-time faculty at those institutions. Little research has attempted to document this increase, however, and the

NSOPF data offer few clues. Yet, a greater use of teaching assistants might have provided one of the escape valves that allowed student-faculty ratios to increase, as noted above, without the expected pressure on educational quality.

The second question has to do with the changing nature of students, particularly the oft-noted growth during the past two decades in the numbers of non-traditional students, older students and those enrolling part-time (Barbett & Korb, 1995; O'Brien, 1992). Edmondson (1997) suggests that new student demographics are already causing a segmentation of higher education into four distinct markets, requiring new approaches to institutional planning and staffing. It may be that the increased hiring of part-time and adjunct faculty observed in the current data is a natural institutional response to the needs of part-time and older students for more flexible course scheduling or for curricula that are less rigidly tied to traditional disciplines and degree programs. If such a link between new student demographics and new faculty hiring patterns could be established, it might be useful for refining projections of demand for PhDs, based on projections of enrollments by category.

Yet, it may be that little of this demographic shift is taking place among students in 4-year institutions at all. Recent IPEDS data show that the percentage of FTE enrollments at 4-year institutions that were made up by part-time students grew by only one percentage point, from 12% to 13%, between 1975 and 1994. The percentage peaked in 1994, and has remained at 12% from 1995 to 1997 (U.S. Department of Education, 2000). Most of the growth in part-time enrollments has occurred at 2-year institutions, outside our purview. Moreover, because all of Bowen and Sosa's estimates, as well as those presented here, employ full-time equivalent (FTE) enrollment figures, the part-time trend has no direct effect on our interpretations of the model and data. Did Bowen and Sosa's underestimation of the college participation rates of older segments of the population contribute to their overall underprojection of liberal arts enrollments? Certainly, but no more than did their underestimation of the participation rates of younger segments. As we have seen, the enrollment projections were the source only of numerical, not theoretical flaws in the model, and relatively blameless ones at that.

Another comment that should be made at the outset is that it is easy to find fault in hindsight, much more difficult to improve on the actual performance the next time around. I have been able to point out the glaring failures in the theoretical and numerical assumptions made in Bowen and Sosa's model, but this stops far short of offering alternative assumptions that could have been employed more effectively at the time. This is because, for the most part, theoretical assumptions are made for the sake of computability, not out of simplemindedness, while numerical assumptions are made by rarely more sophisticated methods than extending or reversing current trends, and thus are inevitably more a matter of luck than skill. The danger of all mathematical models of complex systems like labor markets is that their construction forces us to favor the predictive power of the computable factors (such as enrollments) over the unknowable ones (such as state budgets), even though past experience and theory both argue for the reverse.

Bowen and Sosa did not believe, for example, that older PhD holders never returned to academia, or that faculty size would be completely determined by enrollments alone. Rather, they calculated that other contributing factors were likely to be either too small to make a significant difference, or else too complex to be modeled feasibly. Moreover, their numerical assumptions, such as "the production of new Ph.D.'s will continue unchanged at the 1987 levels," were not attempts at prophesy, but simply admissions that they had no reasonable basis on which to make any other assumptions about the future value of the quantity. The only fair question, therefore, is not "what did they do wrong" but rather, what could we do differently if we were to attempt a new projection today? Undoubtedly, we would fiddle around the edges a bit, tweaking this or that computation or coefficient, but still be prey, in the end, to the same uncertainties.

Indeed, the foregoing analysis does indicate some ways to increase the sensitivity of the model. One of these, for example, would be to improve the validity of the use of degrees by discipline as proxy for enrollments by discipline, thereby increasing the accuracy of the calculations of student-faculty ratios. This could be done by measuring the actual percentages of course enrollments by discipline for each of the different categories of degree seekers at different types of institutions. Such a task would involve a considerable amount of transcript analysis, but would yield a simple matrix of coefficients for converting the numbers of degrees by discipline into estimates of course enrollments by discipline. An easier, and perhaps no less effective method, would be to follow the example of Goldman and Massy's (2001) model of supply and demand for science and engineering doctorates. Goldman and Massy used a measure of the total number of undergraduate degrees awarded by the institutions, distinct from the number of degrees awarded in each discipline of interest, as an indicator of the demand for teaching created by the general-education requirements of students whose degrees would eventually be in other areas. This measure, combined with the direct measure of degrees awarded in the disciplines, would help to give a fuller picture of actual teaching demands generated by overall enrollments both inside and outside the liberal arts.

Another, similar improvement would be to eliminate the assumption that the distribution of tenure would remain constant within each age group for the purpose of calculating quit rates. One could develop a new set of quit rates that took into account both age and tenure status, or age and the number of years at the institution, to allow the quit projections to respond to changes in the average age of new hires. Another adjustment would be to seek a more accurate measure of the intent to pursue an academic career, to replace the "percentage of new PhDs with definite employment plans in the United States who had job commitments in higher education" as proxy for the academic share of new PhDs. This improvement could involve a refinement of items on the SED designed to indicate labor force expectations; combining it with a model of the recent job placement records for PhDs within individual disciplines, disaggregated by institutional sectors, might further refine such a measure. This may prove the most difficult, however. For, as Ehrenberg (1991) amply demonstrates, there is a great deal that we still do not know about the career choices and expectations of doctoral students.

Although each of the adjustments suggested above would improve the model by enhancing the accuracy of its numerical assumptions, the more important conclusions to be drawn from this analysis are those that point to the relative importance of the main components of the model and its vulnerability to the failure of its larger, theoretical assumptions. The labor market data show, for example, that replacement demand is the single most important factor to get right in projecting the balance of supply and demand for faculty. This component of demand, as Bowen and Sosa themselves emphasized and the actual data confirmed, overwhelms the net new positions demand. More importantly, it also overwhelms fluctuations in enrollments. The analysis has shown that even guessing correctly on the dramatic growth of arts and science enrollments would not have contributed much to the accuracy of Bowen and Sosa's projections. The reason is that, contrary to Bowen and Sosa's theoretical assumption about the functioning of academic institutions as hiring and decision-making organizations, colleges and universities clearly acted on factors other than enrollments when making decisions about replacement and hiring of full-time faculty.

The labor market data also show that Bowen and Sosa's theoretical assumptions about the functioning of academic labor markets introduce further weaknesses into the model. Contrary to the assumption that only newly awarded PhDs will make up the supply of new faculty, we saw that significant numbers of new hires were made from the ranks of older PhD holders. Thus, it is clear that some attempt to estimate and account for the backlog of older PhD recipients who hold nonacademic positions now, but may seek academic positions if openings arose, would significantly improve the model's ability to predict faculty supply. Future models of academic labor markets would certainly benefit from the use of an inventory-attrition model like that employed by Cartter (1976, and described above). More immediately, the analysis presented here suggests that policymakers concerned with the optimal size of graduate programs should consider not just the number of expected openings in a discipline 6 or 7 years hence, but also the backlog of current PhD holders who are likely to compete for those openings.

A final example of a possible improvement to the model comes from Goldman and Massy's (2001) study. In contrast to Bowen and Sosa's fixed-coefficient model of the entire national system for arts and sciences, Goldman and Massy constructed a dynamic simulation of labor market and institutional behavior focusing on individual academic departments in science and engineering. As such, their work is not, technically, a projection of future supply and demand so much as an attempt to understand the dynamics of the major forces influencing the labor market in the past (during the 1980s). Using Markov simulation methods, it models some of the important feedback loops and market adjustments that Bowen and Sosa had to ignore. For example, classical labor economics suggests that a depressed job market for PhDs in a specific discipline should result in fewer new applicants to those PhD programs, with the effect of reducing the imbalance after a certain time-lag (Freeman, 1989). Goldman and Massy modeled this effect but found it to be too small to significantly reduce the imbalances they identified. They also modeled the function of departmental choice in optimizing the mix among faculty, post-docs and doctoral students to meet the research and teaching needs of the department, subject to the constraints of research budgets and the number of applicants to doctoral programs. This enabled them to account for the dual role of doctoral students both as additions to the future supply of faculty (as PhDs) and as reductions to the present demand for faculty (as teaching and research assistants), a significant advantage of the dynamical systems approach over the fixed-coefficient model. Goldman and Massy's working hypothesis was that doctoral program size, and hence the eventual supply of PhDs, is determined not by any output labor market considerations, but rather by departmental needs for RAs and TAs, limited only by the financial constraints of supporting the doctoral students. Their simulation results, which confirmed this hypothesis, could be used to improve further the theoretical assumptions of Bowen and Sosa's model. They clearly urge the inclusion of research funding, as well as enrollments, among the drivers of faculty hiring.

Unfortunately, as a practical matter, there may be no accurate way to project such budgets. Moreover, it is not clear how well Goldman and Massy's system could be adapted to making projections across the liberal arts disciplines. In most of the Humanities, for example, the linkages they identified among research budgets, faculty hiring, and doctoral student admissions probably do not apply. Goldman and Massy's recognition, however, that doctoral students supply a significant part of the teaching needs of a department, reducing the demand for PhD faculty, could be used to improve the accuracy Bowen and Sosa's model. Indeed, the analysis presented here suggests that expanding Bowen and Sosa's concept of "faculty" to include part-time and nontenure-track appointments, as well as TAs, would be the most significant single improvement to make in the model. Unfortunately, there is currently no good measure of either the number of TAs employed or the amount of teaching they perform in U.S. universities, with which to implement such an improvement.

This sort of discussion begs the question, however, of whether such massive forecasting efforts as Bowen and Sosa conducted are ultimately worth doing at all, when they so often seem to come out wrong. Bowen and Sosa themselves maintained that their projections would never be observed, because individuals, institutions and markets would all make adjustments in the intervening years. Yet, it is surely too facile to cite Cartter's (1976) self-exonerating claim that a good projection *should* turn out to be a bad prediction by virtue of its success at inducing responsible actors to address the problem at hand, because a wrong projection can be worse than no projection at all if it is so severe or alarmist that the response turns out to be worse than the cause. This would certainly seem to be the case if we were to credit Bowen and Sosa's projection with having lured tens of thousands of the nation's brightest students into lengthy doctoral programs on the promise of plentiful jobs in academia, only to leave them with dashed expectations, embittered outlooks, part-time employment, and many thousands of dollars of debt. Rubenstein (1999) goes so far as to accuse Bowen and Sosa, among others, of acting in bad faith by waging a "skills-shortage campaign," whose hidden agenda was access to cheap labor for industry and academe but whose result has been a wasteful overproduction of PhDs and underconsumption of scholarship. I would not venture so far as Rubenstein, but I am not sure that we would not have been better off today without *Prospects for Faculty*. The question is not without immediate relevance, for if we follow the pattern of major labor market projections in recent decades, we are already due for the next one. Given the lessons learned, I wonder whether we should blithely forge ahead with another, even given the refinements I have recommended.

I suggest that we must. There is a definite need for projections that would enable actors on both sides of the market, institutions and prospective faculty alike, to plan rationally for their futures. Insinuations of bad faith aside, the real danger seems to lie not so much in being wrong, but in being taken too literally. Bowen and Sosa recognized all too well how easy it is to lull readers into complacency with the reassuring precision of numbers, charts and tables. One cannot say often enough, it seems, that the product is merely a hypothetical model based on projections of existing trends, not a prediction of what will actually occur. It may be, therefore, that the best way to improve such models is to do a better job of laying every assumption bare to the reader. To make all of the technical refinements and improvements one can, certainly, but also to make them explicit, and adjustable on the fly. One could envision, for example, the next edition of *Prospects for Faculty* being published as an interactive web-based system, in which the user would have the ability to manipulate independently each of the coefficients in the calculations and watch the resulting effects on the projections instantly take shape. This would have the doubly beneficial effect of, first, allowing each numerical assumption to be adjusted as new data become available and second, allowing users to explore their own "what if" scenarios to see just how speculative the entire exercise truly is.

*Notes*

[1]Reconstructing the playing field of *Prospects for Faculty* has been a relatively straightforward task when using the same series of datasets and surveys that Bowen and Sosa used, namely the National Research Council's annual SDR and SED data and National Center for Education Statistics' (NCES) IPEDS data. Exact correspondences were sometimes more elusive when working with data from the two NSOPF studies, which nonetheless provide much richer snapshots of faculty characteristics. In those cases where the differences were small enough as to be meaningless in the context of comparing relative trends in quantities over time, minor correction factors were introduced into the data in order to match the latest Bowen and Sosa figures (usually 1987) with those from the same year in the current datasets. In all extractions of data from national surveys, weighted estimates were used where appropriate.

[2]These calculations assume that one part-time faculty member is equivalent to 0.56 full-time faculty members, a factor derived from the ratio of the number of courses taught by part-time vs. full-time faculty in NSOPF '93.

*References*

Barbett, S. F., & Korb, R. A. (1995). *Enrollment in higher education: Fall 1984 through Fall 1993* (NCES 1995–04–00).

Barkume, M. (1996–97, Winter). The job market for Ph.D.'s: Two views. *Occupational Outlook Quarterly, 40,* 2–15.

Blum, D. (1991, February 20). Many studies of future academic job market are said to be of little use to policy makers. *Chronicle of Higher Education, 37,* pp. A15, A19.

Bowen, H. R., & Schuster, J. H. (1986). *American professors: A national resource imperiled.* New York: Oxford University Press.

Bowen, W. G., & Rudenstine, N. L. (1992). *In pursuit of the PhD.* Princeton: Princeton University Press.

Bowen, W. G., & Sosa, J. A. (1989). *Prospects for faculty in the arts and sciences: A study of factors affecting demand and supply, 1987 to 2012.* Princeton: Princeton University Press.

Brodie, J. M. (1995, January-February). Whatever happened to the job boom? *Academe, 81,* 12–15.

Burke, D. L. (1988). *The new academic marketplace.* Westport, CT: Greenwood Press.

Caplow, T., & McGee, R. J. (1977). *The academic marketplace* (Reprint of 1958 ed.). New York: Arrow Press.

Cartter, A. M. (1976). *Ph.D.'s and the academic labor market: A report prepared for the Carnegie Commission on Higher Education.* New York: McGraw-Hill.

Chatman, S., & Jung, L. (1992). Concern about forecasts of national faculty shortages and the importance of local studies. *Research in Higher Education, 33,* 31–57.

Clark, B. R. (1987). *The academic life: Small worlds, different worlds* . Princeton: Carnegie Foundation for the Advancement of Teaching.

Edmondson, B. (1997, March). Keeping up with demographic change: Higher education at the start of the next century. *College Board Review, 180,* 24–30.

Ehrenberg, R. G. (1991). Academic labor supply. In C. T. Clotfelter, R. G. Ehrenberg, M. Getz, & J. J. Siegfried (Eds.), *Economic challenges in higher education* (pp. 143–258). Chicago: University of Chicago Press.

El-Khawas, E. (1990). *Campus trends, 1990* (Higher Education Panel Report No. 80). Washington, DC: American Council on Education.

El-Khawas, E. (1991). *Campus trends, 1991* (Higher Education Panel Report No. 81). Washington, DC: American Council on Education.

Fairweather, J. S. (1995). Myths and realities of academic labor markets. *Economics of Education Review, 14,* 179–192.

Finnegan, D. E. (1993). Segmentation in the academic labor market: Hiring cohorts in comprehensive universities. *Journal of Higher Education, 64,* 621–656.

Freeman, R. B. (1989). *Labor markets in action: Essays in empirical economics.* Cambridge: Harvard University Press.

Freeman, R. B. (1999). It's better being an economist (but don't tell anyone). *Journal of Economic Perspectives, 13*(3), 139–145.

Gill, J. I. (1992). *Bringing into focus the factors affecting faculty supply and demand: A primer for higher education and state policymakers.* Boulder, CO: Western Interstate Commission for Higher Education.

Goldman, C. A., & Massy, W. F. (2001). *The PhD Factory: Training and employment of science and engineering doctorates in the United States.* Bolton, MA: Anker Publishing.

Hansen, W. L. (1985). Changing demography of faculty in higher education. In S. M. Clark & D. R. Lewis (Eds.), *Faculty vitality and institutional productivity: Critical perspectives for higher education* (pp. 27–54). New York: Teachers College Press.

Hartle, T. W., & Galloway, F. J. (1996, September/October). Too many PhDs? Too many MDs? *Change, 28,* 26–33.

Holden, K. C., & Hansen, W. L. (Eds.). (1989). *The end of mandatory retirement: Effects on higher education.* San Francisco: Jossey-Bass.

Kelley, M. R., Pannapacker, W., & Wiltse, E. (1998, December 18). Scholarly associations must face the true causes of the academic job crisis [Opinion]. *Chronicle of Higher Education, 45,* p. B4.

Kirshstein, R. J., Matheson, N., & Jing, Z. (1997). *Instructional faculty and staff in higher education institutions: Fall 1987 and Fall 1992* (Statistical Analysis Report ): National Center for Education Statistics, US Department of Education.

Lozier, G. G., & Dooris, M. J. (1987, November). *Is higher education confronting faculty shortages?* Paper presented at the annual meeting of the Association for the Study of Higher Education, Baltimore.

McGinnis, R., & Long, J. S. (1988). Entry into academia: Effects of stratification, geography and ecology. In D. W. Breneman & T. I. K. Youn (Eds.), *Academic labor markets and careers* (pp. 28–51). New York: The Falmer Press.

McGuire, M. D., & Price, J. A. (1989). *Faculty replacement needs for the next 15 years: A simulated attrition model.* Paper presented at the 29th annual forum of the Association for Institutional Research, Baltimore.

Mortimer, K. P., Bagshaw, M., & Masland, A. T. (1985). *Flexibility in academic staffing: Effective policies and practices* (ASHE-ERIC Higher Education Report No. 1). Washington, DC: Association for the Study of Higher Education.

National Center for Education Statistics. (1998). *The condition of education, 1998.*

National Center for Education Statistics DAS data access system [http://nces.ed.gov/das/]:

National Science Foundation WebCASPAR data access system [http://caspar.nsf.gov]:

Nerad, M., & Cerny, J. (1999). Postdoctoral patterns, career advancement, and problems. *Science, 285,* 1533–1535.

O'Brien, E. M. (1992). Part-time enrollment: Trends and issues. *ACE Research Briefs, 3*(8).

Pollak, M. (1999, September 15). Ph.D.'s fault universities' roles in helping them to find work. *New York Times,* p. B10.

Rosenfeld, R. A., & Jones, J. A. (1988). Exit and re-entry in higher education. In D. W. Breneman & T. I. K. Youn (Eds.), *Academic labor markets and careers* (pp. 74–97). New York: The Falmer Press.

Rubenstein, E. S. (1999, Fall). Piled Higher and deeper: The alleged shortage of highly educated workers in the U.S. is a myth. *American Outlook,* 44–47.

Sanderson, A., Dugoni, B., Hoffer, T., & Selfa, L. (1999). *Doctorate recipients from United States universities: Summary report 1998.* Chicago: National Opinion Research Center (The report gives the results of data collected in the Survey of Earned Doctorates, conducted for five Federal agencies, NSF, NIH, NEH, USED, and USDA, by NORC.).

Schuster, J. H. (1995, Fall). Whither the faculty? The changing academic labor market. *Educational Record,* 28–33.

Tuckman, H. P., & Pickerill, K. M. (1988). Part-time faculty and part-time academic careers. In D. W. Breneman & T. I. K. Youn (Eds.), *Academic labor markets and careers* (pp. 98–113). New York: The Falmer Press.

U.S. Department of Education. (2000). *Digest of Education Statistics, 1999.* Washington, DC: National Center for Education Statistics.

Youn, T. I. K. (1988). Studies of academic labor markets and careers: A historical review. In D. W. Breneman & T. I. K. Youn (Eds.), *Academic labor markets and careers.* New York: The Falmer Press.

Lamont Flowers
Steven J. Osterlind
JE Ernest T. Pascarella
Christopher T. Pierson

# How Much Do Students Learn in College?

## Cross-Sectional Estimates Using the College BASE

*Introduction*

What students learn during the undergraduate years in postsecondary education has been the focus of a large body of inquiry for the past 30 years (e.g., Bowen, 1977; Gardner, 1994; Kuh, Douglas, Lund, & Ramin-Gyurnek, 1994; Osterlind, 1997; Pascarella & Terenzini, 1991; Stage, Muller, Kinzie, & Simmons, 1998). The vast majority of these studies document the change, or growth, that occurs between the first and subsequent years of college. Overall, this research has taken three different forms. The first form is longitudinal (or panel) studies that trace changes in the same students over time on some standardized, objective measure of cognitive development or knowledge (e.g., critical thinking, mathematical reasoning, literacy, history, science reasoning). The average change between the freshman and senior year of college, for example, might then be an estimate of the impact of college. Recent examples of studies of this type are by Baxter Magolda (1990, 1991), Giancarlo and Facione (1997), Hart, Rickards, and Mentkowski (1995), King and Kitchner (1994), Kube and Thorndike (1991), May (1990), Saucier (1995), Thorndike, Andrieu-Parker, and Kube (1990), Thorndike and Andrieu-Parker (1992), and Zhang and RiCharde (1999).

The second form is cross-sectional (or cohort) studies that administer

*Lamont Flowers is assistant professor in the Department of Educational Leadership, Policy, and Foundations at the University of Florida; Steven J. Osterlind is professor of educational psychology at the University of Missouri; Ernest T. Pascarella is the Mary Louise Petersen Chair in Higher Education at the University of Iowa; and Christopher T. Pierson is a doctoral student in higher education and law student at the University of Iowa. (Authorship is in alphabetical order.)*

*The Journal of Higher Education,* Vol. 72, No. 5 (September/October 2001)
Copyright © 2001 by The Ohio State University

some standardized objective measure of cognitive development or knowledge to students with different levels of exposure to postsecondary education. For example, one might administer the same instrument at the same time to first-year students and seniors and assume that the difference between the average scores of the two groups is an estimate of the impact of college. Recent examples of this type of study are found in ACT (1993), Durham, Hays, and Martinez (1994), Evans (1989), Hill (1995), Jehng, Johnson, and Anderson (1993), King and Kitchener (1994), McDonough (1997), Osterlind (1997), Pearson and Rogers (1998), and Wood (1997).

The third form of study employs students' retrospective self-reports of how much they change or gain along various dimensions of knowledge or cognitive development during college. The assumption, not without some empirical support (e.g., Anaya, 1999a, 1999b; Bradburn & Sudman, 1988; Trusheim, 1994), is that students will be both truthful and accurate in responding to such instruments. Recent examples of this type of study are by Bauer (1996, 1998), Dollar (1991), Feldman (1994), Lincoln (1991), Tan (1995), and Williams (1996).

Each of these three popular forms of research provides legitimate approaches to understanding the change and growth in knowledge and cognitive development that occur during college, and in the clear majority of cases they report statistically significant and sometimes sizable indications of growth or change. Yet, if one is interested in estimating the net impact of college (i.e., how much of what happens is attributable to the experience of college and not to coincident or competing influences, or measurement error), then each of these forms of research is also limited. For example, longitudinal panel studies of change during college have the problem of not knowing whether similar students who do not attend college might also change to the same or to a similar extent. Additionally, there is the problem of the practice effect (part of the change from the first to subsequent testings may be due simply to students taking the test more than once and not to the impact of college).

Cross-sectional or cohort studies have their own methodological problems too. Probably the most important as an estimate of the impact of college is concerned with sample mortality. Because of sample mortality, seniors might represent a more academically select and motivated group than first-year students. Thus, higher average scores by seniors versus first-year students, for example, might reflect comparison group differences in academic aptitude and motivation, not simply the impact of college.

Finally, student self-reports of cognitive gains or growth during college are also limited as an estimate of the net impact of college. Probably the major issue in the use of self-reports is their veracity and the question of what it is that they measure. Unfortunately, the correlations between student self-reports and scores on objective, standardized measures are often quite modest in magnitude (e.g., Osterlind, Robinson, & Nickens, 1997; Pascarella & Terenzini, 1991; Pike 1995, 1996; Steel & Nichols, 1992). Although having low correlations with objective, standardized measures of student learning does not necessarily mean that self-reports are psychometrically invalid measures of college impact, this fact might well lead to serious questions about their content or face validity by faculty and administrators. Another important problem centers on disentangling students' self-reports of gains during college from the very characteristics of the students reporting them. For example, if seniors at a selective, residential liberal arts college report greater cognitive gains during college than seniors at a large, state university, the temptation might be to conclude that the former provides a more cognitively impactful environment than the latter. However, students enrolling in selective, residential liberal arts colleges may simply be more open to the cognitive impacts of postsecondary education to begin with than their counterparts enrolling in a large state university. Thus, the differences observed between institutional types might simply reflect differences in the characteristics of the students enrolled and not the unique impact of the institution itself (Kuh, 1993; Pascarella & Terenzini, 1991). Without taking such student background characteristics into account, it is problematic to attribute differences in self-reported cognitive gains by students with different amounts of exposure to college (e.g., sophomores vs. seniors) to the impact of college (Pascarella & Terenzini, 1991).

To be sure, there is a limited body of research that specifically attempts to estimate the net impact of college on learning or cognitive development by introducing controls for important student background characteristics (e.g., Flowers & Pascarella, 1999; Kitchener, 1992; Myerson, Rank, Raines, & Schnitzler, 1998; Pascarella, 1989; Pascarella, Bohr, Nora, & Terenzini, 1996; Rykiel, 1995; Smith-Sanders & Twale, 1997, 1998; Whitmire & Lawrence, 1996; Wolfle, 1983). The results of these studies clearly suggest that, even in the presence of statistical controls for important student background characteristics (e.g., academic ability, motivation, race, sex, high-school performance) students with more exposure to postsecondary education make greater gains in measures of learning or cognitive development than students with less or no exposure.

However, this small body of research also has a number of distinct limitations. First, with a few exceptions there is little evidence concerning the actual magnitude or size of the net impacts of college. Pascarella

(1989), and Pascarella, et al. (1996) analyzing data from two independent samples report a net advantage in critical thinking of about 0.4 of a standard deviation, but this estimate is limited to the impact of exposure to the first year of college. A second and related problem is that there is little or no information about the timing of the net impacts of college on learning or cognitive growth. Does most of the impact occur early during one's exposure to postsecondary education, or are the impacts spread more evenly across the undergraduate experience? Finally, there is little evidence on whether the net impacts of college on learning or cognitive development are general or conditional. That is, are the impacts essentially similar in magnitude for all students (i.e., general effects) or do they differ in magnitude for students with different background characteristics (e.g., academic ability, race, gender), or for students in different institutional contexts (e.g., the average academic ability of the student body)? The latter are termed conditional effects.

This study sought to address these problems in the existing research by analyzing a large, multi-institutional sample of freshmen, sophomores, juniors, and seniors who completed the *College Basic Academic Subjects Examination* (hereafter CBASE) (Osterlind, 1997). The study had three specific purposes. First, it sought to estimate the magnitude of the effects of year in school on CBASE scores with controls for important individual student precollege characteristics (e.g., academic ability, race, gender), as well as the context of the institution in which the student was enrolled (e.g., an estimate of average academic ability of the institution's student body). Second, by estimating the relative net effects of year in school, the analyses yielded evidence with regard to when the largest effects occurred in a student's undergraduate experience. Third, the study sought to determine the presence of conditional effects of year in college on CBASE scores. That is, do the net effects of college differ in magnitude for students with different precollege characteristics, or for students in different institutional contexts?

## Methodology

### Initial Sample

The data for the study came from undergraduate students enrolled in 56 four-year colleges and universities located in 13 states. The institutions were both public and private and consisted of liberal arts colleges, regional colleges and universities, and research universities. About 25% of the institutions were doctorate-granting universities. The students at each institution came from all classes, freshman through senior, and agreed to participate in an assessment conducted by their institution.

Thus, there was no random sampling strategy used to form the sample. All students were tested between 1993 and 1998, although there were only a small percentage in the years 1993 and 1998; hence the vast majority were tested between 1994 and 1997. Most participants in the sample were full-time students between the ages of 19 to 22, and as a group had a racial composition that approximated the national distribution for four-year institutions. Thus, despite the fact that the sample was not scientifically drawn, it nevertheless had reasonable comparability with a national profile of full-time, traditional-age college students.

*Instrument*

The measure of student learning used in the study was the *College Basic Academic Subjects Examination* or CBASE (Osterlind, 1997). The CBASE is a standardized measure of scholastic achievement in four content areas: English, mathematics, science, and social studies. In addition, the test assesses three reasoning competencies across the disciplines: interpretive reasoning, strategic reasoning, and adaptive reasoning. The model underlying these cognitive–processing competencies is based on the theoretical work of Hannah and Michaelis (1997). Organizationally, the CBASE is divided into four sections; each one devoted to a particular content subject. The content subjects themselves are divided into two or three "clusters" of skills for that area. The English test is composed of the two clusters reading and literature, and writing; the mathematics test is composed of the three clusters general mathematics proficiency, algebra, and geometry; the science test is made up of the two clusters laboratory and field work, and fundamental concepts; and the two clusters history and social sciences compose the social studies test. In all, nine clusters aggregate into the four CBASE subject tests. The clusters are themselves further subdivided into a number of "enabling subskills." For example, reading critically, reading analytically, and understanding literature are enabling subskills within the cluster called "reading and literature." Similarly, evaluating algebraic and numerical expressions, and solving equations and inequalities are enabling subskills within the cluster called "algebra." In total the exam includes four subject areas, nine clusters, and 23 skills.

The main focus of the test is on CBASE scores in the four content areas (i.e., English, mathematics, science, and social studies) plus a Composite score that combined all four subject tests. Evidence for valid score interpretation yielded by the CBASE is evident through a number of sources, following guidelines set forth in the Standards for Educational and Psychological Testing (American Psychological Association,

1985). Perhaps most important is information pertinent to the content validity of the instrument. The CBASE has a written rationale and a detailed plan for development. Extensive test specifications exist. These test specifications were prepared over a period of one year with advice from more than 100 content experts, primarily from universities throughout the country. Separate studies with appropriate college-level populations were conducted to determine congruence with other measures (e.g., the ACT and SAT) as well as for scaling and test standardization. The four content areas were developed through factor analysis and item analysis for individual test items (including bias and differential performance). According to independent studies of the use of the four content area scores, the CBASE can be employed to assess student knowledge and skills and to evaluate the quality and effectiveness of academic programs (Pike, 1991, 1992). In the present study the correlations between the four CBASE subject scores and students' cumulative college grades ranged from 0.22 to 0.30. The correlation between the Composite score and cumulative grades in college was 0.32. The alpha, internal consistency reliabilities for the four CBASE tests are: English 0.77, mathematics 0.89, science 0.78, and social studies 0.83.

*Variables*

The study had five dependent variables, including the four subject scores on the CBASE (i.e., English, mathematics, science, and social studies), and a composite score that combined all four subject tests. The independent variable was year in school (i.e., freshman, sophomore, junior, or senior). Because it was anticipated that sample mortality effects might bias upward the estimated effects of year in school on CBASE scores (e.g., seniors being a more academically select group than freshmen), controls for a number of important confounding variables were introduced. At the individual level controls were made for three precollege or demographic variables: academic ability (self-reported composite ACT score or SAT equivalent), sex, and race (i.e., African American, Latino, Asian American, Native American, and Caucasian). A series of preliminary analyses also included age, but its unique relationship with CBASE scores, and its contribution to the results, was so trivial that it was excluded. Also included were two additional individual-level control variables. The first was self-reported total credit hours taken in postsecondary education. It was judged important to include this variable to have at least some control for possible academic coursework taken at other institutions prior to the one at which the student was when he or she took the CBASE. The second was self-reported cumulative grade point average during college. Because grades appear to measure academic motivation and willingness to work hard as well as academic ability (Pascarella & Terenzini, 1991), it was thought important to control for cumulative grade point average as a reasonable proxy for a student's level of academic motivation.

Because evidence also suggests that the overall cognitive or academic ability of an institution's student-body can influence the climate of an institution (Astin, 1977, 1993; Pascarella & Terenzini, 1991), an estimate of aggregate student-body academic ability was also included as a control variable. This estimate was the mean self-reported ACT or SAT equivalent of the students enrolled in each institution in the study. Each individual student was then assigned the mean estimate of student-body academic aptitude at his or her institution.

Although it would have been preferable to have actual rather than self-reported measures of academic aptitude and college grades, there is clear evidence of a high correspondence on these measures. For example, Trusheim (1994) found correlations between self-reported scores and actual scores of 0.93 and 0.94 for SAT Verbal and SAT Quantitative scores, respectively. Similarly, reviewing nearly 40 years of research, Baird (1976) found that correlations between self-reported and actual grades ranged from 0.74 to 0.96. Furthermore, in our sample the self-reported measures appeared to have simple correlations with CBASE scores that were both reasonable in magnitude and consistent with previous evidence (e.g., Pascarella & Terenzini, 1991). For example, the self-reported ACT score had simple correlations with the CBASE composite score that ranged between 0.51 and 0.52, while the estimated institutional average ACT score had correlations with the CBASE composite score that ranged between 0.21 and 0.22. Self-reported college grades had correlations with the CBASE composite score that ranged between 0.30 and 0.32.

*Final Sample*

The study sample was comprised of students from 56 four-year postsecondary institutions with complete data on all variables. Only those institutions were included that had tested a minimum of 50 students, although because of the distribution, the effective minimum number of students was closer to 90. This yielded effective samples of 19,717 for the English test; 19,363 for the mathematics test; 19,461 for the science test; 19,848 for the social studies test and 18,418 in analyses of CBASE Composite. The sample was approximately 53% seniors, 17% juniors, 16% sophomores, and 14% freshmen.

*Analyses*

The primary analyses regressed each of the five CBASE scores on the set of six control variables (i.e., individual ACT score; race; sex; cumulative grade point average; total postsecondary credits taken; average institutional ACT score), and year in college. Race was represented by dummy variables representing African American, Asian American, Latino, and Native American, with Caucasian always coded 0. Year in college was represented by dummy variables for sophomore, junior, or senior, with freshman always coded 0. Thus, all resulting coefficients for year in college represented comparison with freshman students or those with the least exposure to postsecondary education. The unstandardized regression coefficient, or $b$, for sophomores, juniors, or seniors indicated the advantage (versus freshmen) on CBASE subject scores, net of the confounding variables. A separate set of regressions was also run to determine the unique variance increment ($R^2$ increase) attributable to year in college. These regressions were conducted in a setwise manner with all six of the control variables entered on step one, and the three dummy variables representing year in college entered on a subsequent step.

To determine the magnitude of the effects of year in college on CBASE scores, two "effect sizes" were estimated. The first, suggested by Hays (1994), divided the unstandardized regression weight ($b$) for sophomores, juniors, and seniors by the pooled sample standard deviation of the dependent variable. The resultant effect size represented that part of a standard deviation on specific CBASE subject scores that sophomores, juniors, or seniors were advantaged relative to their freshman counterparts. Computation of a second effect size was recommended by a reviewer. In this effect size estimate the $b$ weight for year in college was divided by the square root of the mean square residual for the overall regression equation. Because this approach takes into account the reduction in the residual variance ($1-R^2$), it produces effect sizes that are larger than those produced when the $b$ weight is divided by the pooled standard deviation of the dependent variable. One might consider our first approach to estimating effect size as providing a conservative estimate, whereas our second approach provides a more liberal estimate.

Before conducting the primary analyses of the study we sought to determine if the net effects of year in college differed in magnitude for students in different categories or different levels of the six control variables (i.e., individual ACT scores, sex, race, cumulative grade point, total postsecondary credits taken, average institutional ACT score). As indicated previously, these are termed "conditional effects." A set of cross-product terms was developed between the six control variables and the three dummy variables representing year in college. This set of cross-product terms was then added to the regression equations specified in the primary analyses (i.e., the six control variables plus the three dummy variables representing year in college). A significant increase in $R^2$ (explained variance) due to the set of cross-product terms indicated the presence of significant conditional effects for year in college (Pedhazur, 1982). If this condition was met, we then determined the significance of specific conditional effects in two steps. First, we determined if each specific conditional effect (for example, the set of three cross-product terms representing the conditional effect of individual ACT score x year in college) accounted for a significant $R^2$ increase over and above all main effects plus the set of cross-products representing all other conditional effects (Pedhazur, 1982). Second, we also determined if each specific conditional effect accounted for a significant increase in $R^2$ over and above the main effects.

Because of the extremely large sample sizes, a conservative alpha level was chosen. No effect was considered significant unless the null hypotheses could be rejected at $p < 0.001$.

## Results

The overall tests for the presence of conditional effects were significant at $p < 0.001$ for all five dependent measures. The addition of the entire set of control variable x year in college cross-products to the main-effect equations were associated with $R^2$ increases of between 0.92% and 1.20%. However, only one conditional effect (sex x year in college) met both tests for the significance of an individual conditional effect. Controlling for all main effects and all other conditional effects, the three cross-product terms representing sex x year in college were associated with modest, but significant ($p < 0.001$) $R^2$ increases across all five dependent variables of between 0.65% and 0.90%. Similarly, with all main effects in the equation the three cross-product terms representing sex x year in college accounted for significant ($p < 0.001$) $R^2$ increases across all five dependent variables of between 0.70% and 0.95%. None of the other conditional effects met either of these criteria, even at $p < 0.05$. Such evidence suggests that the effects of college on CBASE scores did not differ in magnitude for students who differed in precollege academic ability, race, college grades, cumulative credits taken in postsecondary education, or the average academic ability of the students at the institution attended. On the other hand, the significant sex x year in college conditional effect suggests that the effects of college on

CBASE scores differ in magnitude for men and women. Consequently, we disaggregated the sample by sex and developed separate estimates for men and women.

Table 1 summarizes the estimates of net effects of each year in college (versus freshmen) on CBASE scores for men and women. The table shows a number of general trends. First, using the Composite score as a reasonable average of the four subject area scores, estimates of the overall net effects of college indicate that senior men have between 0.7 and 0.9 of a standard deviation advantage over freshman men, and senior women have between 0.5 and 0.6 of a standard deviation advantage over freshman women across all CBASE subject scores. These are typically considered moderate to large size effects (e.g., Bowen, 1977).

A second major trend supported in the data is that the vast majority of college impact on CBASE scores appears to take place during the first two years of college. This is evident from comparisons of the magnitude of the sophomore (versus freshman) effect sizes with the corresponding magnitudes of the senior (versus freshman) effect sizes. Again, using the Composite score as a reasonable average of the four subject area scores, it was found that the estimated sophomore effect for men, of between 0.708 and 0.868 of a standard deviation, was about 95% of the estimated senior effect for men, of between 0.742 and 0.909 of a standard deviation. Similarly, the corresponding average sophomore effect for women, of between 0.487 and 0.596 of a standard deviation, was about 98% of the estimated senior effect for women, of between 0.496 and 0.608 of a standard deviation.

Simply looking at the Composite score, however, does mask some interesting patterns of estimated effects attributable to year in college. For example, on both the English and social studies tests most of the estimated net effect of the college experience does occur by the sophomore year. However, students also appear to make modest additional progress in these areas through their senior year. On the English test, for example, the estimated sophomore (versus freshman) effect sizes for men and women ranged between 84% and 71% of the corresponding senior (versus freshman) effect sizes for men and women, respectively. Similarly, on the social studies test, the estimated sophomore effect sizes for women were about 75% of the corresponding senior (versus freshman) effect sizes. For both men and women on the English test, and for women on the social studies test, the unstandardized regression coefficients ($b$) for the estimated sophomore and senior effects were significantly different from each other at $p < 0.001$.

A different pattern for the net effects of the college experience emerged for the mathematics and science tests. On the mathematics test,

TABLE I

Estimated Effects of College on CBASE Scores for Men and Women

| Year in College | English | | Mathematics | | Science | | Social Studies | | Composite | |
|---|---|---|---|---|---|---|---|---|---|---|
| | Men | Women | Men | Women | Men | Women | Men | Women | Men | Women |
| **Sophomore (vs. Freshman)** | | | | | | | | | | |
| b | 38.230 | 24.700 | 33.500 | 27.400 | 44.130 | 31.450 | 36.070 | 20.160 | 39.840 | 27.390 |
| Effect size estimate I[a] | 0.612 | 0.396 | 0.488 | 0.400 | 0.603 | 0.430 | 0.559 | 0.313 | 0.708 | 0.487 |
| Effect size estimate II[b] | 0.718 | 0.464 | 0.586 | 0.474 | 0.716 | 0.510 | 0.663 | 0.371 | 0.868 | 0.596 |
| Women's effect size as a percent of men's effect size | 64.70 | | 81.79 | | 71.31 | | 55.90 | | 68.79 | |
| **Junior (vs. Freshman)** | | | | | | | | | | |
| b | 38.410 | 24.880 | 27.740 | 21.490 | 43.780 | 34.310 | 35.470 | 19.240 | 39.170 | 27.150 |
| Effect size estimate I[a] | 0.616 | 0.399 | 0.404 | 0.313 | 0.598 | 0.469 | 0.550 | 0.298 | 0.696 | 0.483 |
| Effect size estimate II[b] | 0.721 | 0.467 | 0.485 | 0.376 | 0.709 | 0.556 | 0.652 | 0.353 | 0.853 | 0.591 |
| Women's effect size as a percent of men's effect size | 64.77 | | 77.48 | | 78.43 | | 54.20 | | 69.40 | |
| **Senior (vs. Freshman)** | | | | | | | | | | |
| b | 45.630 | 35.070 | 36.390 | 15.280 | 43.500 | 30.510 | 38.430 | 26.850 | 41.740 | 27.900 |
| Effect size estimate I[a] | 0.731 | 0.561 | 0.531 | 0.223 | 0.595 | 0.417 | 0.596 | 0.416 | 0.742 | 0.496 |
| Effect size estimate II[b] | 0.857 | 0.659 | 0.631 | 0.266 | 0.705 | 0.495 | 0.708 | 0.494 | 0.909 | 0.608 |
| Women's effect size as a percent of men's effect size | 76.74 | | 42.10 | | 70.15 | | 69.80 | | 66.84 | |
| Pooled Standard Deviation | 62.43 | | 68.58 | | 73.15 | | 64.51 | | 56.24 | |
| Square root of pooled mean square residual | 53.21 | | 57.18 | | 61.67 | | 54.39 | | 45.92 | |
| $R^2$ Total Model | 0.247 | 0.285 | 0.272 | 0.299 | 0.255 | 0.289 | 0.217 | 0.261 | 0.354 | 0.395 |
| $R^2$ Increase Due to Year in College | 0.021 | 0.015 | 0.012 | 0.013 | 0.016 | 0.016 | 0.016 | 0.010 | 0.024 | 0.019 |

NOTES: Controls: ACT score; Race (African American, Asian American, Caucasian, Latino, Native American); College grades; Cumulative credits taken in postsecondary education; Average ACT score of the sample of students at the institution attended. All estimated effects (i.e., b, $R^2$ Total Model, $R^2$ Increase Due to Year in College) are statistically significant at $p < 0.001$.

[a] divided by sample pooled standard deviation.

[b] divided by square root of pooled mean square error from regression including main effects and cross-product terms for conditional effects.

the estimated sophomore (versus freshman) effect sizes for women were actually somewhat larger than the corresponding senior (versus freshman) effect sizes for women (about 1.8 times as large). Indeed, the *b* weight representing the sophomore effect for women (27.40) was significantly ($p < 0.001$) larger than the corresponding *b* weight representing the senior (versus freshman) effect for women (15.28). Thus, the estimates suggest that after making substantial progress in mathematics during the first two years of college (between 0.400 and 0.474 of a standard deviation) women tend to retrogress through their senior year. Despite this slipping backward, senior women are still functioning at about a quarter (0.223 to 0.266) of a standard deviation higher in mathematics than are freshman women. For men about 92% of the senior advantage over freshmen in mathematics comes by the end of the sophomore year. However, the estimated senior advantage over freshmen (0.531 to 0.631 of a standard deviation) is still larger, though not significantly so, than the advantage of sophomore men over their freshman counterparts (0.488 to 0.586 of a standard deviation).

On the science test, the progress made during the first two years of college by both men and women appears to stabilize and remain largely unchanged throughout the remainder of college. There was a general parity between the estimated sophomore (versus freshman) and senior (versus freshman) effects on science knowledge for both men and women. In both cases the b weight for the sophomore effect (44.13 for men and 31.45 for women) was not significantly different from the *b* weight for the senior effect (43.50 for men and 30.51 for women).

Finally, as suggested by the modest, but statistically significant sex x year of enrollment conditional effects across all five CBASE scores, there were non-chance differences in the effects of college for men and women. As Table 1 suggests, the impact of college on CBASE scores was substantially more pronounced for men than it was for women. Using the CBASE Composite score as a reasonable average across the four subject areas, the data from Table 1 clearly indicate that the estimated sophomore, junior, and senior (versus freshman) effect sizes for women were only about two-thirds (around 67%), of the corresponding effect sizes for men. If one considers the senior (versus freshman) net difference as an estimate of the overall effect of college, senior men had between 0.742 and 0.909 of a standard deviation advantage on the CBASE composite over their freshman counterparts. Senior women, on the other hand, had a net advantage over freshman women of between 0.496 and 0.608 of a standard deviation on the CBASE Composite score. The ratio of the senior (versus freshman) effect sizes for men and women on the both the science and social studies tests averaged about

0.70, or 70%; and the corresponding ratio of the senior effect sizes for men and women on the English test was about 0.77 or 77%. On the mathematics test, however, the advantage of senior women over their freshman counterparts was only about 42% of the corresponding advantage of senior men over freshman men. In light of such evidence it may be that men are making greater learning gains during college than women are, at least as measured by the CBASE.

## Conclusions and Discussion

This study employed a cross-sectional design with statistical controls for important confounding influences to estimate the net impact of college on five standardized, objective measures of learning: English, mathematics, science, social studies, and a composite of all four tests. The findings suggest a number of general conclusions. First, estimates from samples of students attending 56 four-year colleges and universities suggest that, on average, across all subject areas, senior men have an advantage of between 0.74 and 0.91 of a standard deviation over freshman men. Senior women had an average advantage across all subject areas of between 0.50 and 0.61 of a standard deviation over their freshman counterparts. These are typically considered moderate to large effects, and they persisted net of statistical controls for individual ACT score, race, college grades, total credits taken in postsecondary education, and the average ACT score of students at the institution attended. For both men and women the estimated net effects of college varied among subject areas, from relatively smaller senior (versus freshman) advantages in mathematics (0.22 to 0.27 of a standard deviation for women and 0.56 to 0.63 of a standard deviation for men) to relatively larger corresponding advantages in English (0.56 to 0.66 of a standard deviation for women and 0.73 to 0.86 of a standard deviation for men).

A second major finding was that there were statistically significant differences by sex in the magnitude of the effects of college on CBASE scores. Our estimates suggest that the cognitive impacts of college may be substantially more pronounced for men than for women. Indeed, on average, across all subject areas, the net sophomore, junior, and senior (versus freshman) effects for women were only 69%, 69%, and 67% of the respective sophomore, junior, and senior (versus freshman) effects for men. In the senior year this ratio of female/male effects (expressed as a percentage) ranged from a low of about 42% in mathematics, to a high of about 77% in English.

Estimates using the CBASE would tend to support the contention that postsecondary education is a "gendered experience" that is not only manifestly different for women but may also be structured toward masculine rather than feminine intellectual orientations and learning styles (e.g., Baxter Magolda, 1992, 1998; Belenky, Clinchy, Goldberger, & Tarule, 1986; Hall & Sandler, 1982; Holland & Eisenhart, 1990; Levine & Cureton, 1998; Seymore, 1995; Whitt, 1992). To the extent this is the case, there may be sex-based classroom, organizational, or environmental differences woven into the fabric of postsecondary institutions that lead to women making smaller knowledge gains than men. For example, recent evidence from analyses of the National Study of Student Learning suggests that both classroom and nonclassroom actions that are perceived as unsupportive of women can have negative consequences for women's academic and cognitive growth during college (e.g., Pascarella, Whitt, Edison, Nora, Hagedorn, Yeager, & Terenzini, 1997; Whitt, Edison, Pascarella, Nora, & Terenzini, 1999). It is difficult to determine the influence of such factors from the CBASE data, however, because, unlike the National Study of Student Learning database, it does not contain extensive information regarding student classroom or nonclassroom experiences.

Of course there is an obvious alternative hypothesis to explain the gender differences we found in the effects of college on CBASE scores. Men and women tend to enroll in different majors (Jacobs, 1996; Pascarella & Terenzini, 1991), and attendant differences in coursework taken might well account for some, if not all, the differences we observed, particularly in mathematics and science. Although this possibility is indeed acknowledged, it is important to point out that the overall impact of college for women (i.e., the senior versus freshman effect) was significantly and substantially smaller than that for men across all the CBASE subject tests. Still, because the CBASE data do not contain information on major field of study or coursework taken, we cannot determine the extent to which such factors may have accounted for the gender differences we observed. This is a clear limitation of our study.

A third major finding from our estimates was that the vast preponderance of college impact on CBASE subject areas occurred during the first two years of postsecondary education. On average, across all subject tests, the net sophomore-freshman difference was about 95% to 98% of the net senior-freshman difference. There was modest continued improvement in English and social studies through the senior year; but on science there was little or no improvement, and on mathematics the net senior-freshman difference for women was actually smaller than the corresponding sophomore-freshman difference. Because the CBASE is designed to assess knowledge and intellectual skills learned as a result of general education courses, this overall trend is perhaps not surprising.

For students who do not major in quantitative fields most required mathematics courses may be completed in the first two years of college. Findings by Wolfle (1983) suggest that for those who do not major in quantitative fields, college tends to stabilize mathematical competencies at the levels at which students enter college. Our findings are in partial agreement with Wolfle's, but in the CBASE sample men and women had respective senior-year mathematics scores that were between 0.53 and 0.63 of a standard deviation, and between 0.22 and 0.27 of a standard deviation greater than those of their freshman counterparts.

A fourth major finding of the study was what was *not* found. Recall that tests for conditional effects indicated that, net of the control variables, including individual level ACT scores, the effect of college on CBASE scores did not differ for students who attended institutions differing in the average ACT scores of their student bodies. Put another way, the cognitive impact of college did not differ in magnitude for students attending institutions differing in academic selectivity. (Although our institutional sample did not include institutions of the very highest selectivity [such as Ivy League institutions] there was still a substantial amount of heterogeneity in average institutional ACT score. The estimated average institutional ACT range in the sample was about 18.50 to 28.10.) Such results are quite consistent with recent findings reported by Hagedorn, Pascarella, Edison, Braxton, Nora, & Terenzini (1999). They found that the average level of measured critical thinking of the students at an institution had no significant effect on growth in individual student critical thinking after three years of college. Our estimates are also consistent with the conclusion of Pascarella & Terenzini (1991) in their review of 20 years of research on the impact of college on students; namely, institutional selectivity, in and of itself, may have only trivial and inconsistent net impacts on the cognitive development or learning gains of individual students. Institutions that have relatively stringent admissions standards may not always provide the most impactful intellectual environment. Programmatic efforts and the quality of teaching may be more salient determinants of an institution's impact on student learning and cognitive growth than the average academic selectivity of the student body.

## References

Anaya, G. (1999a). *Accuracy of student-reported test scores: Are they suited for college impact assessment?* Unpublished manuscript, Indiana University, Bloomington, IN.

Anaya, G. (1999b). College impact on student learning: Comparing the use of self-reported gains, standardized test scores, and college grades. *Research in Higher Education, 40,* 499–526.

American College Testing Program (1993). *CAAP user norms: Fall, 1993.* Iowa City, IA: Author.

American Psychological Association. (1985). *Standards for educational and psychological testing.* Washington, DC: Author.

Astin, A. (1977). *Four critical years.* San Francisco: Jossey-Bass.

Astin, A. (1993). *What matters in college.* San Francisco: Jossey-Bass.

Baird, L. (1976). *Using self-reports to predict student performance.* Research Monograph No. 7. New York: College Entrance Examination Board.

Bauer, K. (1996, May). *Year two of the longitudinal study of university undergraduates: Changes occurring from the freshman to sophomore year.* Paper presented at the meeting of the Association for Institutional Research, Albuquerque, NM.

Bauer, K. (1998, May). *Academic and social development of undergraduate students: Summary of findings for the UD longitudinal study, Fall 1993–Spring 1997.* Paper presented at the meeting of the Association for Institutional Research, Minneapolis, MN.

Baxter Magolda, M. (1990). Gender differences in epistemological development. *Journal of College Student Development, 31,* 555–561.

Baxter Magolda, M. (1991, April). *A gender inclusive model of epistemological development.* Paper presented at the annual meeting of the American Educational Research Association, Chicago.

Baxter Magolda, M. (1992). *Knowing and reasoning in college: Gender-related patterns in students' intellectual development.* San Francisco: Jossey-Bass.

Baxter Magolda, M. (1998). Measuring gender differences in intellectual development: A comparison of assessment methods. *Journal of College Student Development, 29,* 528–537.

Belenky, M., Clinchy, B., Goldberger, N., & Tarule, J. (1986). *Women's ways of knowing: The development of self, voice, and mind.* New York: Basic Books.

Bowen, H. (1977). *Investment in learning.* San Francisco: Jossey-Bass.

Bradburn, N., & Sudman, S. (1988). *Polls and surveys.* San Francisco: Jossey-Bass.

Dollar, R. (1991). College influence on analytical thinking and communication skills of part-time versus full-time students. *College Student Journal, 25,* 273–279.

Durham, R., Hays, J., & Martinez, R. (1994). Socio-cognitive development among Chicano and Anglo American college students. *Journal of College Student Development, 35,* 178–182.

Evans, D. (1989). Effects of a religious-oriented, conservative, homogeneous college education on reflective judgment. *Dissertation Abstracts International, 49,* 3306-A.

Feldman, M. (1994). A strategy for using student perceptions in the assessment of general education. *Journal of General Education, 43,* 151–167.

Flowers, L., & Pascarella, E. (1999). Cognitive effects of college racial composition on African American students after three years of college. *Journal of College Student Development, 40,* 669–677.

Gardner, L. (1994). *Redesigning higher education: Producing dramatic gains in student learning.* Washington, DC: Clearinghouse on Higher Education, The George Washington University.

Giancarlo, C., & Facione, P. (1997). *A longitudinal study of Santa Clara undergraduate students' dispositions toward critical thinking.* Unpublished manuscript, Santa Clara University, Santa Clara, CA.

Hagedorn, L., Pascarella, E., Edison, M., Braxton, J., Nora, A., & Terenzini, P. (1999). Does institutional context influence the development of critical thinking? A research note. *Review of Higher Education, 22,* 247–263.

Hall, R., & Sandler, B. (1982). *The campus climate: A chilly one for women?* Report of the Project on the Status and Education of Women. Washington, DC: Association of American Colleges.

Hannah, L., & Michaelis, J. (1977). *A framework for instructional objectives: A guide to systematic planning and evaluation.* Reading, MA: Addison-Wesley.

Hart, J., Rickards, W., & Mentowski, M. (1995, April). *Epistemological development during and after college: Longitudinal growth on the Perry scheme.* Paper presented at the annual meeting of the American Educational Research Association, San Francisco.

Hays, W. (1994). *Statistics (5th ed.).* Fort Worth, TX: Harcourt Brace College Publications.

Hill, D. (1995). Critical thinking and its relation to academic, personal, and moral development in the college years. *Dissertation Abstracts International, 56,* 4603-B.

Holland, D., & Eisenhart, M. (1990). *Educated in romance: Women, achievement, and college culture.* Chicago: University of Chicago Press.

Jacobs, J. (1996). Gender inequity and higher education. *Annual Review of Sociology, 22,* 153–185.

Jehng, J., Johnson, S., & Anderson, R. (1993). Schooling and students' epistemological beliefs about learning. *Contemporary Educational Psychology, 18,* 23–35.

King, P., & Kitchener, K. (1994). *Developing reflective judgment.* San Francisco: Jossey-Bass.

Kitchener, K. (1992). *The development of critical reasoning: Does a college education make a difference?* (University Lecture). Denver, CO: University of Denver.

Kube, B., & Thorndike, R. (1991). *Cognitive development during college: A longitudinal study measured on the Perry scheme.* Paper presented at the annual meeting of the American Educational Research Association, Chicago, IL.

Kuh, G. (1993). In their own words: What students learn outside the classroom. *American Educational Research Journal, 30,* 277–304.

Kuh, G., Douglas, K., Lund, J., & Ramin-Gyurnek, J. (1994). *Student learning outside the classroom: Transcending artificial boundaries.* ASHE-ERIC Higher Education Report No. 8. Washington, DC: George Washington University, School of Education and Human Development.

Levine, A., & Cureton, J. (1998). *When hope and fear collide.* San Francisco: Jossey-Bass.

Lincoln, C. (1991). The relation between college orientation and student effort: An exploratory study. *Dissertation Abstracts International, 51,* 4034–A.

May, D. (1990). *Student development: A longitudinal investigation of the relationship between student effort and change in intellectual development.* Unpublished doctoral dissertation, Memphis State University, Memphis, TN.

McDonough, M. (1997). An assessment of critical thinking at the community college level. *Dissertation Abstracts International, 58,* 2516-A.

Myerson, J., Rank, M., Raines, F., & Schnitzler, M. (1998). Race and general cognitive ability: The myth of diminishing returns to education. *Psychological Science, 9,* 139–142.

Osterlind, S. (1997). *A national review of scholastic achievement in general education: How are we doing and why should we care?* ASHE-ERIC Higher Education Report Volume 25, No. 8. Washington, DC: The George Washington University, Graduate School of Education and Human Development.

Osterlind, S., Robinson, R., & Nickens, N. (1997). Relationship between collegians' perceived and congeneric tested achievement in general education. *Journal of College Student Development, 38,* 255–265.

Pascarella, E. (1989). The development of critical thinking: Does college make a difference? *Journal of College Student Development, 30,* 19–26.

Pascarella, E., Bohr, L., Nora, A., & Terenzini, P. (1996). Is differential exposure to college linked to the development of critical thinking? *Research in Higher Education, 37,* 159–174.

Pascarella, E., & Terenzini, P. (1991). *How college affects students: Findings and insights from twenty years of research.* San Francisco: Jossey-Bass.

Pascarella, E., Whitt, E., Edison, M., Nora, A., Hagedorn, L., Yeager, P., & Terenzini, P. (1997). Women's perceptions of a "chilly climate" and their cognitive outcomes during the first year of college. *Journal of College Student Development, 38,* 109–124.

Pearson, F., & Rodgers, R. (1998). Cognitive and identity development: Gender effects. *Initiatives, 58,* 17–33.

Pedhazur, E. (1982). *Multiple regression in behavioral research: Explanation and prediction* (2nd ed.). New York: Holt, Rinehart & Winston.

Pike, G. (1991). Assessment measures. *Assessment Update: Progress, Trends, and Practices in Higher Education, 3*(1), 6–7.

Pike, G. (1992). The components of construct validity: A comparison of two measures of general education outcomes. *Journal of General Education, 41,* 130–160.

Pike, G. (1995). The relationship between self-reports of college experiences and achievement test scores. *Research in Higher Education, 36,* 1–21.

Pike, G. (1996). Limitations of using students' self-reports of academic achievement measures. *Research in Higher Education, 37,* 89–114.

Rykiel, J. (1995). The community college experience: Is there an effect on critical thinking and moral reasoning? *Dissertation Abstracts International, 56,* 3824-A.

Saucier, B. (1995). Critical thinking skills of baccalaureate nursing students. *Journal of Professional Nursing, 11,* 351–357.

Seymore, E. (1995). The loss of women from science, mathematics, and engineering undergraduate majors: An exploratory account. *Science Education, 79,* 437–473.

Smith-Sanders, C., & Twale, D. (1997, March). *Impacts of number and type of core curriculum hours on critical thinking.* Paper presented at the annual meeting of the American Educational Research Association, Chicago, IL.

Smith-Sanders, C., & Twale, D. (1998, March). *Further study of the impact of number and type of core curriculum hours on critical thinking.* Paper presented at the annual meeting of the American Educational Research Association, San Diego, CA.

Stage, F., Muller, P., Kinzie, J., & Simmons, A. (1998). *Creating learning centered classrooms: What does learning theory have to say?* (ASHE-ERIC Higher Education Report, No. 4.) Association for the Study of Higher Education.

Steel, J., & Nichols, P. (1992, November). *Linking COMP objective test scores with student perceptions of growth.* Paper presented at the annual meeting of the American Evaluation Association, Seattle, WA.

Tan, D. (1995). Do students accomplish what they expect out of college? *College Student Journal, 29,* 449–454.

Thorndike, R., & Andrieu-Parker, J. (1992, April). *Growth in knowledge: A two-year longitudinal study of changes in scores on the College Basic Academic Subjects Examination.* Paper presented at the annual meeting of the American Educational Research Association, San Francisco, CA.

Thorndike, R., Andrieu-Parker, J., & Kube, B. (1990, April). *Impact of college experiences on cognitive development.* Paper presented at the annual meeting of the American Educational Research Association, Boston, MA.

Trusheim, D. (1994). How valid is self-reported financial aid information? *Research in Higher Education, 35,* 335–348.

Whitmire, E., & Lawrence, J. (1996, November). *Undergraduate students' development of critical thinking skills: An institutional and disciplinary analysis and comparison with academic library use and other measures.* Paper presented at the annual meeting of the Association for the Study of Higher Education, Memphis, TN.

Whitt, E. (1992, November). *"Taking women seriously": Lessons for coeducational institutions from women's colleges.* Paper presented at the Annual Meeting of the Association for the Study of Higher Education, Minneapolis, MN.

Whitt, E., Edison, M., Pascarella, E., Nora, A., & Terenzini, P. (1999). Women's perceptions of a "chilly climate" and cognitive outcomes in college: Additional evidence. *Journal of College Student Development, 40,* 163–177.

Williams, R. (1996). Assessing students' gains from the college experience at East Tennessee State University. *Dissertation Abstracts International, 57,* 970–A.

Wolfle, L. (1983). Effects of higher education on achievement of blacks and whites. *Research in Higher Education, 19,* 3–9.

Wood, P. (1997). A secondary analysis of claims regarding the Reflective Judgment Interview: Internal consistency, sequentiality, and intro-divisional differences in ill-structured problem solving. In J. Smart (Ed.), *Higher education: Handbook of theory and research* (Vol. 12, pp. 243–312). New York: Agathon.

Zhang, Z., & RiCharde, R. (1999). Intellectual and metacognitive development of male college students: A repeated measures approach. *Journal of College Student Development, 40,* 721–738.

## ꟻE Laura W. Perna

# The Relationship Between Family Responsibilities and Employment Status Among College and University Faculty

Although the participation of mothers in the labor force is viewed more favorably now than in the past, a substantial proportion of American workers continue to believe that women should focus their efforts on the home (Bond, Galinsky, & Swanberg, 1997). For example, surveys by the Families and Work Institute revealed that 41% of employees nationwide agreed in 1997 that men should be the breadwinner and women should care for the home and children, down from 64% in 1977 (Bond, Galinsky, & Swanberg, 1997).

Research suggests that college and university faculty also perceive tension between work and family roles (Cole & Zuckerman, 1987; Finkel, Olswang, & She, 1994; Marshall & Jones, 1990; Sorcinelli & Near, 1989). For instance, from their exploratory study of 12 women and minorities who had made choices about entering academia, Bronstein, Rothblum, and Solomon (1993) concluded that the concentration of women in nontenure-track and part-time positions was due, in part, to the conflict between career and family demands. Through interviews, Cole and Zuckerman (1987) found that even the youngest women scientists in their sample, women who had received their doctorates during the 1970s, encountered individuals who viewed marriage and motherhood to be incompatible with a scientific career. Although Marshall and Jones (1990) found that the timing of childbearing was unrelated to salaries and academic rank among female higher education deans, ad-

The author is grateful for the comments and suggestions of Jeffrey Milem and three anonymous reviewers.

*Laura W. Perna is assistant professor, Department of Education Policy and Leadership, University of Maryland at College Park.*

*The Journal of Higher Education,* Vol. 72, No. 5 (September/October 2001)

ministrators, and counselors, they also found that about two-thirds of their sample believed that childbearing had negatively affected their careers, particularly in terms of their professional advancement and mobility. A survey of tenured and tenure-track faculty at one university showed that the majority (70%) believed that taking leave after the birth of a child would be detrimental to their careers (Finkel et al., 1994).

The lower representation of married women than single women, and women with children than childless women, among the nation's college and university faculty may also suggest the difficulties associated with fulfilling both family and career responsibilities. Analyses of the 1993 National Study of Postsecondary Faculty (NSOPF:93) reveal that women represent a smaller share of married than never married faculty (34% versus 52%) and a smaller share of faculty with children than childless faculty (31% versus 54%). Some research (e.g., Cooney & Uhlenberg, 1989) suggests that these patterns are similar to those for other professional women. For example, using 1980 census data, Cooney and Uhlenberg (1989) showed that White women lawyers, physicians, and postsecondary teachers were substantially less likely than White women of the same age in the general population to be married and have children. Among White women between the ages of 35 and 39 with at least ten years of marriage, a substantially higher share of postsecondary teachers than of physicians or lawyers were childless (Cooney & Uhlenberg, 1989).

Although the challenges associated with balancing work and family roles may not be unique to faculty, these data raise important questions not only about the extent to which marriage and motherhood may limit access to a faculty career in general but also about the specific types of academic positions that are available to married women and women with children. Of particular concern is the extent to which married women and women with children may be concentrated in lower-status faculty positions. Although the representation of women among college and university faculty has increased since the mid-1970s, the greatest growth has been among part-time and nontenure-track appointments (Chronister, Gansneder, Harper, & Baldwin, 1997; Lomperis, 1990). While the number of nontenured but tenure-track full-time faculty increased between 1976 and 1993 at a faster rate for women than men (22% increase for women versus 24% decline for men), the greatest growth has been among non-tenure track appointments. Between 1976 and 1993, the number of non-tenure track full-time faculty increased by 142% for women and 54% for men (Chronister et al., 1997). In part because of these differential growth rates, analyses of the NSOPF:93 show that women represented a higher share of full-time, nontenure-track faculty than of full-time, tenure-track faculty in fall 1992 (52% versus 43%).

Although anecdotal evidence (e.g., Flynn, Flynn, Grimm, & Lockhart, 1986; Wilson, 1998) suggests that not all nontenure-track faculty are dissatisfied with their status, many nontenure-track faculty may be considered to be marginal "in the sense that they hope for full integration into academe" (Bowen & Schuster, 1986, p. 65), and because they represent a lower rung on the hierarchy of academic labor markets (Youn, 1992). According to Youn (1992), the existence of hierarchies within the academic labor market contributes to various forms of segmentation including segmentation by job status (e.g., full-time or part-time). Movement from one job status segment to another (e.g., from part-time to full-time or from nontenure-track to tenure-track) is restricted, just as is movement from one academic discipline to another (e.g., from mathematics to English). Competition among faculty in different segments is limited, thereby permitting inequities among faculty across segments (Youn, 1992).

This study uses data from the NSOPF:93 to explore the extent to which the higher observed representation of women among nontenure-track faculty (i.e., the lower status positions) is related to family responsibilities after taking into account other variables that are expected to be related to employment status. Sex differences in the relationship between family responsibilities and employment status are examined and implications of the findings are discussed.

*Theoretical Framework*

Although little is known about the relationship between family responsibilities and employment status among college and university faculty, researchers have explored the relationship between family responsibilities and such outcomes as research productivity and salaries. From her comprehensive review and synthesis of prior research, Creamer (1998) concluded that most research shows no relationship between marital status and publishing productivity for women. In fact, some evidence suggests that married faculty are more productive than other faculty after controlling for other differences (Bellas & Toutkoushian, 1999). Some researchers (e.g., Astin & Bayer, 1979; Astin & Davis, 1985) have shown that married women, and others (e.g., Bellas, 1992; Hamovitch & Morgenstern, 1977) have shown that married men are more productive than their single counterparts of the same sex. The extent to which the occupation of the spouse is related to scholarly productivity is equivocal. Using a national sample of faculty employed at colleges and universities in 1989, Astin and Milem (1997) found that, after controlling for differences in background and job-related characteristics, having an academic spouse was associated with higher levels of research productivity for women but lower levels of research productivity for men. In contrast, using a sample of faculty employed in the state of Illinois in 1993, Bellas (1997b) found that having an academic partner was unrelated to research productivity after taking into account differences in other variables.

With regard to the relationship between parental responsibilities and research productivity, Creamer (1998) also concluded from her review of prior research that the relationship is ambiguous. She found no significant relationship between having children and publishing productivity in five of the ten studies reviewed, a positive relationship in three of the ten, and a negative relationship in two of the ten. Using a subsample from the NSOPF:93, Bellas and Toutkoushian (1999) showed that full-time faculty with dependents had higher levels of research productivity than full-time faculty without dependents after controlling for differences in sex, race, education, experience, academic field, institutional type, and allocation of time.

In terms of the relationship between family responsibilities and faculty salaries, Johnson and Stafford (1974), using data from the 1970 National Science Foundation Register, showed that labor force participation among women faculty was influenced by marital status, husband's earnings, and number of children and that time out of the labor force for child bearing and child rearing was negatively related to earnings. Whereas Barbezat (1988), after controlling for other variables, found marital status to be unrelated to the salaries of women and men faculty in both 1968 and 1977, others have shown that married men faculty received higher salaries than their single male counterparts in both 1984 (Bellas, 1992) and 1992 (Toutkoushian, 1998). Some research (Bellas, 1992; Astin & Milem, 1997) suggests that the employment status of the spouse or partner also matters. Bellas (1992) found that men faculty with nonemployed wives averaged higher salaries than men faculty with employed wives even after controlling for education, experience, productivity, rank, institutional characteristics, and academic field. Astin and Milem (1997) found that, after controlling for differences in background and job-related characteristics, having an academic spouse was associated with higher salaries among women faculty but lower salaries among men faculty. Some research (Barbezat, 1988) indicates that men faculty, but not women faculty, with children receive higher salaries.

In one of the few examinations of the relationship between family responsibilities and employment status, Ferber and Hoffman (1997) found that neither the probability of being employed at a research or doctoral

university nor the probability of holding the highest rank of full professor were related to such measures of household responsibilities as geographic distance from the current partner, number of years spent with
partners, level of education of partners, number of years partners employed at the same institution, number of children, and number of years
children spent in the household among women faculty employed at colleges and universities in the state of Illinois in 1993.

Prior research has drawn upon two perspectives to examine gender
equity issues in academic employment: human capital and structural.
According to human capital theory, an individual's status and rewards in
the academic labor market are determined primarily by his or her productivity. Productivity is expected to be determined by the investments
that individuals make in themselves, particularly the quantity and quality of their education and the amount of their on-the-job training, as well
as their geographic mobility, their motivation and intensity of work, and
their emotional and physical health (Becker, 1962, 1993).

Some economists have argued that family responsibilities influence
investment in human capital, continuity of labor force participation,
types of employment sought, and level of commitment to the job
(Becker, 1985; Polachek, 1977). Even today family responsibilities continue to be borne primarily by women (Bond et al., 1997). For example,
a 1997 national survey of workers in a variety of occupations showed
that married employed women spent more time than married employed
men caring for their children and engaging in household chores on both
workdays and non-workdays (Bond et al., 1997).

With regard to the accumulation of human capital, an individual who
is out of the labor force because of family responsibilities is not acquir-
ing additional on-the-job experience and may even be losing some previously acquired job skills (Becker, 1993). Korenman and Neumark
(1991) noted that most prior research has concluded that children reduce
wages indirectly by reducing labor force participation and the "accumulation of human capital" (e.g., experience) rather than by directly reducing productivity. Arguing that prior estimates may be biased, however,
Korenman and Neumark (1991) concluded that children may directly reduce women's wages and that, because of this reduction in wages,
women reduce their participation in the labor market. Regardless of the
direction of causality, women with children appear to average lower levels of experience.

Family responsibilities may also reduce geographic mobility. Research has shown that women are less mobile than men (Marwell,
Rosenfeld, & Spilerman, 1979; Rosenfeld & Jones, 1987). For example,
women have been found to be more likely than men to remain in the

geographic area where they attended graduate school and to be concentrated in larger urban areas where, presumably, the probability of both partners finding satisfactory employment is higher (Marwell et al., 1979; Rosenfeld & Jones, 1987). The advantages of geographic mobility are evidenced by research showing that faculty who are more mobile receive higher salaries (Astin & Bayer, 1979; Smart & McLaughlin, 1978; Kasten, 1984), are more likely to hold tenure track positions (Rosenfeld & Jones, 1987), and tend to hold higher academic rank (Marwell et al., 1979) than other faculty.

Family responsibilities may also be related to the level of motivation and intensity of work. Human capital theorists (e.g., Becker, 1985) predict that, compared with men and single women, married women pursue less demanding jobs, such as part-time and nontenure-track positions, because household responsibilities require more effort than leisure and other nonmarket activities and, consequently, they have less energy available for market work. In other words, differences in household responsibilities are expected to be associated with differences in motivation and intensity of work and are expected to lead to occupational segregation by sex (Becker, 1985).

Marriage and parenting responsibilities may also influence emotional and physical health. As Tack and Patitu (1992) observed from their comprehensive review of the predictors of job satisfaction among women and minority faculty, "life-style stressors" (e.g., child care, parent care, physical and mental health) likely have a stronger impact on women than men because of societal expectations about the priority women should place on their families. Some (Austin & Pilat, 1990) have speculated that women may also feel greater stress and pressure than men in their attempts to balance work and family responsibilities because of the physical demands of pregnancy, childbirth, and early parenthood.

Household responsibilities and children's problems have been shown to be more important sources of stress for women faculty than for men faculty (Dey, 1994). Among full-time tenure-track faculty at one university, 28% more women than men reported experiencing at least one of the following conflicts between work and child care: avoiding overnight conferences because of child care demands, bringing a child to the university, delaying promotion or tenure because of child care responsibilities, or being unavailable to attend a function at the child's school because of work demands (Riemenschnieder & Harper, 1990). About two-thirds of women faculty, but only one-third of men faculty, reported feeling overwhelmed trying to meet both child care and employment demands (Riemenschnieder & Harper, 1990). Findings from another single institution study suggest that women faculty are as involved with their work as men, but that women are more likely than men to forego leisure activities in order to satisfy work-related demands (Sorcinelli & Near, 1989).

Despite the popularity of human capital theory for explaining differences in labor market experiences, some economists and sociologists have noted the limitations of this theory (DeYoung, 1989; Dreijmanis, 1991). Such critics argue that "focusing on the supply of human skills to explain economic inequality and lack of productivity is a theoretical mistake" (DeYoung, 1989, p. 155). Among the limitations is the inability of human capital theory to adequately explain the lower returns to educational investments among women and minorities (DeYoung, 1989). Based on her examination of the relationship between time out of the labor force and occupational choice, England (1982) concluded that "human capital theory has not generated an explanation of occupational sex segregation that fits the evidence" (p. 358). Contrary to the predictions of human capital theory, England's analyses of data from the National Longitudinal Survey showed that women with more continuous employment histories or plans were no less likely than other women to work in predominantly female occupations, the presumably lower-status occupations. In a test of Becker's (1985) assertion that women seek less demanding jobs and devote less effort to their jobs than men, Bielby and Bielby (1988) found that, after controlling for household responsibilities, earnings, and job responsibilities, women actually allocate more effort to their work than men.

Social scientists interested in the issues of social inequality and poverty have responded to the inadequacies of human capital theory by developing structural or institutional approaches to understanding labor markets (Youn, 1988). This perspective of labor market experiences generally emphasizes the effects of the attributes of the organizations with which individuals are connected, particularly the influence of the characteristics of the colleges and universities in which they were trained and in which they work, including these institutions' financial resources, tenure system, academic governance, and collective bargaining agreements.

Structural models posit that sex differences in the labor market experiences of faculty are attributable to the segregation of women in the types of institutions, academic fields, and work roles that have lower prestige and value (Smart, 1991). For example, Sorenson (1989) found that 20% of the national male-female wage difference in 1983 for all occupations, not just for faculty or higher education positions, was attributable to occupational segregation by sex after controlling for personal characteristics (e.g., tenure on the job, educational attainment, and full- or part-time status), characteristics of the occupation (e.g., education and training required to perform the job and working conditions), and attributes of the firm (e.g., geographic region, union status, size of firm, and major industry category). In higher education, the average salaries of faculty in institutions and disciplines with higher proportions of women have also been found to be lower than the average salaries of faculty in institutions and disciplines with smaller proportions of women (Barbezat, 1988; Bellas, 1994, 1997a; Smart, 1991).

*Research Method*

Although researchers have examined the effects of marital and parental status on research productivity and salaries, little is known about the relationship between family responsibilities and the employment status of faculty. Given the recent growth in nontenure-track positions, such research is particularly timely. Because some (e.g., Smart, 1991) have concluded that substantial research supports the appropriateness of both human capital and structural approaches to academic labor markets, this study draws upon both perspectives to explore the following research questions:

1. Are family responsibilities related to the employment status of women and men junior faculty after controlling for differences in human capital and structural characteristics?
2. To what extent are junior faculty satisfied holding nontenure-track positions?

*Sample*

Data from the NSOPF:93 are used to address the research questions. Sponsored by the U.S. Department of Education's National Center for Education Statistics, the NSOPF:93 is designed to provide a national profile of faculty, particularly with regard to their professional backgrounds, responsibilities, workloads, salaries, benefits, and attitudes. In the first stage of the two-stage sample selection, 974 public and private nonproprietary higher education institutions were selected and 817 agreed to participate. In the second stage, approximately 42 faculty and instructional staff were selected from each participating institution. A total of 25,780 questionnaires were returned by the 31,354 faculty and instructional staff who were sampled. For additional details on the survey methodology, refer to Kirshstein, Matheson, and Jing (1997).

The sample used in this research is limited to junior faculty whose primary responsibility is teaching. Junior faculty are defined as individuals with faculty status who hold tenure-track or nontenure-track positions. Tenured faculty and faculty who work at colleges and universities that do not have a tenure system are excluded from the sample.

The NSOPF:93 weight (WEIGHT) is appropriate for approximating the population of college and university faculty from the sample. To minimize the influence of large sample sizes and correct for the non-simple random sample design on standard errors, each case is weighted by the NSOPF:93 weight divided by the average weight for the sample (average weight = 37.72). The adjusted weighted sample includes 6,505 cases and represents 245,382 junior faculty nationwide.

### Variables

The hypothesized predictors of employment status include measures of family responsibilities, human capital, and structural characteristics. In addition to sex, four racial/ethnic groups are considered: Black, Hispanic, Asian, and White. White is the reference group. Family responsibilities are measured by marital status and parental status. Marital status is measured by three dichotomous variables: married (married or living with someone); previously married (separated, divorced, or widowed); and never married (reference category). Parental status is measured by whether the individual has at least one child (yes or no).

Human capital is accumulated via educational attainment, on-the-job training, experience, and mobility (Becker, 1962). The level of investment in formal education is measured by a three-level categorical variable: whether an individual holds less than a doctoral degree; whether an individual holds a doctoral degree from a non-Research I university; and whether an individual holds a doctoral degree from a Research I university (reference category). On-the-job training is measured by whether the individual held a research assistantship and/or a teaching assistantship during graduate school. Experience is measured by the number of years since receiving the highest degree and the number of years in the current position (correlation = 0.405). Whether the individual is in his or her first or only job since having earned the highest degree (yes or no) is the best available proxy for mobility.

Structural attributes describe the type of institution and academic discipline in which a faculty member works. A categorical variable reflecting institutional Carnegie classification measures institutional resources as well as occupational segregation by institutional type. The categories are Research I (reference category), other Doctoral, Comprehensive I, other four-year, other (e.g., specialized), and two-year. The existence of collective bargaining agreements is measured by whether the faculty at the institution are unionized (yes or no). A measure of the tenure system, another structural attribute, is not necessary because only junior (i.e., nontenured) faculty working at institutions with a tenure system are included in the analyses. With regard to academic field, 12 categories are included to reflect substantive similarities as well as similarities in the representation of women among junior faculty in the field. The categories are nursing and other health (76% women), English and foreign languages (67%), education (66%), fine arts (49%), psychology, sociology, and other social sciences (48%), biology (38%), mathematics and computer science (33%), business (31%), history, philosophy, law, economics, and political science (31%), first-professional health (30%), engineering and physical science (15%), and other field (40% women). The reference category is engineering and physical science.

### Analyses

The dependent variable, employment status, has four categories: employed full-time on a tenure track; employed part-time on a tenure track; employed full-time, not on a tenure track; and employed part-time, not on a tenure track. Because of the categorical nature of the dependent variable, a multinomial logit model, a special case of the general log-linear model, is used to examine the relationship between family responsibilities and employment status after controlling for human capital and structural characteristics. Part-time, tenure-track faculty are excluded from the multinomial logit analyses for two reasons. First, because the number of cases with part-time, tenure-track employment status is small (adjusted weighted sample size = 131, 2% of all junior faculty), including a separate category for part-time, tenure-track employment would result in problems with zero cells and unstable estimates of coefficients and standard errors (Menard, 1995).

Second, combining part-time, tenure-track with one of the other groups is inappropriate because the descriptive analyses show that part-time, tenure-track faculty are different from other faculty in several respects. Table 1 shows that part-time employment appears to be more common at public two-year institutions regardless of tenure status, with about 44% of part-time, tenure-track and part-time, nontenure-track faculty employed at public two-year institutions. Part-time, tenure-track faculty are relatively less common at Research I universities, with only 3% of part-time, tenure-track faculty but 12% of all junior faculty working at Research I universities. Part-time, tenure track faculty have generally received their highest degrees more recently and have worked fewer years in their current positions than other junior faculty. Though marital status appears to be unrelated to employment status, a higher share of part-time, tenure-track faculty than of all junior faculty have at least one child (78% versus 62%).

Therefore, only three employment categories are considered in the multi-nomial logit model: (1) employed full-time, on a tenure track; (2) employed full-time, not on a tenure track; and (3) employed part-time, not on a tenure track. Two contrasts are possible with three outcome categories. Full-time, nontenure-track employment and part-time, nontenure-track employment are simultaneously contrasted to full-time, tenure-track employment.

Multinomial logit models estimate the log-odds of one outcome oc-

TABLE 1

Selected Characteristics of Women and Men Junior Faculty by Employment Status: Fall 1992

| Characteristic | Total | Full-time Tenure Track | Part-time Tenure Track | Full-time Nontenure Track | Part-time Nontenure Track |
|---|---|---|---|---|---|
| Weighted sample | 245,382 | 4,928 | 87,592 | 35,442 | 117,420 |
| Adjusted weighted *n* | 6,505 | 131 | 2,322 | 940 | 3,113 |
| Distribution | 100.0% | 35.7% | 2.0% | 14.4% | 47.9% |
| INSTITUTIONAL TYPE | 100% | 100% | 100% | 100% | 100% |
| Research I | 12.0% | 11.6% | 3.1% | 17.1% | 11.1% |
| Other doctoral | 14.7% | 19.4% | 13.2% | 19.0% | 10.0% |
| Comprehensive I | 25.2% | 30.1% | 20.2% | 28.4% | 20.7% |
| Other 4-year | 12.3% | 15.3% | 10.1% | 14.5% | 9.4% |
| Public 2-year | 29.7% | 18.4% | 45.0% | 12.1% | 42.8% |
| UNIONIZED INSTITUTION | 44.8% | 41.1% | 51.1% | 41.5% | 48.3% |
| WOMEN | 46.0% | 43.0% | 46.6% | 52.3% | 46.4% |
| MARRIED | | | | | |
| Total | 72.9% | 72.3% | 75.6% | 71.0% | 73.8% |
| Men | 78.1% | 80.0% | 77.1% | 74.2% | 77.8% |
| Women | 66.6% | 62.0% | 73.8% | 67.9% | 69.1% |
| PREVIOUSLY MARRIED | | | | | |
| Total | 12.8% | 12.3% | 9.2% | 12.1% | 13.5% |
| Men | 9.3% | 7.9% | 2.9% | 10.7% | 10.4% |
| Women | 16.9% | 18.1% | 18.0% | 13.6% | 17.2% |
| AT LEAST 1 CHILD | | | | | |
| Total | 62.1% | 62.6% | 77.7% | 58.2% | 62.2% |
| Men | 69.7% | 71.0% | 82.9% | 62.6% | 70.1% |
| Women | 53.1% | 51.5% | 70.5% | 54.2% | 53.1% |
| LESS THAN DOCTORAL DEGREE | | | | | |
| Total | 66.2% | 40.3% | 81.3% | 71.4% | 83.5% |
| Men | 61.0% | 34.6% | 76.5% | 69.2% | 79.4% |
| Women | 72.1% | 47.8% | 86.7% | 73.4% | 88.0% |
| NO. YEARS SINCE HIGHEST DEGREE | | | | | |
| Total | 12.1 | 13.0 | 8.7 | 11.8 | 14.9 |
| Men | 13.0 | 13.8 | 8.9 | 13.6 | 16.1 |
| Women | 11.1 | 12.1 | 8.3 | 10.1 | 13.4 |
| NO. YEARS IN CURRENT POSITION | | | | | |
| Total | 5.5 | 7.7 | 4.2 | 6.0 | 6.2 |
| Men | 6.0 | 8.8 | 4.4 | 6.3 | 7.1 |
| Women | 4.9 | 6.3 | 4.0 | 5.7 | 5.2 |

SOURCE: Analyses of 1993 National Study of Postsecondary Faculty (NSOPF:93).

curring relative to the baseline category (i.e., full-time, tenure track employment). If the baseline category is $J$, the model for the $i^{th}$ category (e.g., full-time, nontenure-track employment) is:

$$\text{Log}(P_i/P_j) = B_{i0} + B_{i1}X_1 + B_{i2}X_2 + ... + B_{ip}X_p$$

The logistic coefficients that result from this equation may be interpreted as the change in log odds associated with a one-unit change in the independent variable. The interpretation of the multinomial logit coefficients is facilitated by the use of odds-ratios, as described by the following equation:

$$P_i / P_j = e^{B_{i0} + B_{i1}X_1 + \ldots + B_{ip}X_p} = e^{B_{i0}} e^{B_{i1}X_1} \cdots e^{B_{ip}X_p}$$

The odds-ratio represents the change in the odds of choosing a particular employment status relative to the reference employment status (full-time tenure-track) that is associated with a one-unit change in a particular independent variable. An odds-ratio greater than one represents an increase in the likelihood of part-time or full-time, nontenure-track employment relative to full-time, tenure-track employment, whereas an odds-ratio less than one represents a decrease in the likelihood of part-time or full-time, nontenure-track employment.

The two continuous variables, number of years since receiving the highest degree and number of years in the current position, are entered into the model as covariates. The test of whether a coefficient is different from zero is based on the Wald statistic, which is calculated as the coefficient divided by its standard error, squared. Goodness-of-fit is reflected by the change in −2 log likelihood. A pseudo-$R^2$ is reported to provide an indication of the strength of the relationship between the outcome variable and the independent variables.

### Limitations

One of the limitations of this study is that the analyses exclude individuals who have chosen not to hold a faculty position. In other words, only individuals who have chosen to try to balance work and family (as evidenced by their presence in the sample) are included in the analyses. Descriptive analyses suggest that comparable proportions of women and men junior faculty are in their prime childbearing years (under age 40) (about 36%). This suggests that women are no more likely than men to "opt out" of faculty careers because they want marriage and parenting to be a part of their lives. Nonetheless, because of the lack of information about qualified individuals who decide not to pursue faculty careers, the findings from this research may underestimate the relationship between family responsibilities and employment status.

A second limitation of this study pertains to the adequacy of the available variables in the database. Although the NSOPF:93 has many strengths, the database includes few direct measures of family responsibilities. Examples of important, but unavailable, variables include the ages of dependent children, timing of childbearing, childcare arrangements, employment status and occupation (e.g., academic or nonacademic) of the spouse, income of the spouse, amount of time spent out of the labor force because of family responsibilities, time devoted to household chores, and time devoted to child care. The NSOPF:93 also lacks measures of parent care-giving, a potentially important influence on employment status given that a 1997 survey found that 25% of the wage and salaried labor force nationwide had elder care responsibilities during the prior year, that employees with elder care responsibilities provided an average of 11 hours per week in assistance, and that 37% of employees with elder care responsibilities took time off from work to provide that assistance (Bond, Galinsky, & Swanberg, 1997). In addition, although holding the first or only job since earning the highest degree may be an inadequate proxy for mobility, the NSOPF:93 lacks appropriate alternative measures.

A third limitation pertains to the difficulty of determining the direction of causality between family responsibilities and employment status using this cross-sectional database. Therefore, this study focuses on exploring the relationship between family responsibilities and employment status among junior faculty, rather than on drawing conclusions about causality. To more fully explore the intercorrelations among the variables in the model, the analytic strategy involves entering conceptually related variables together. Sex and race are entered into the model first. Then family responsibilities are added to determine whether family responsibilities are related to employment status apart from the influence of human capital and structural characteristics. Measures of human capital are then entered into the model, followed by measures of structural characteristics.

## Findings

### Observed Relationships Between Family Responsibilities and Employment Status

The descriptive analyses suggest that women junior faculty hold a relatively higher proportion of full-time, nontenure-track positions and a relatively smaller proportion of full-time, tenure-track positions. Table 1 shows that women represent 52% of full-time, nontenure-track faculty, 47% of part-time, tenure-track faculty, 46% of part-time, nontenure-track faculty, and 43% of full-time, tenure-track faculty.

Regardless of employment status, a smaller proportion of women than men are married (67% versus 78% overall), but a higher proportion of women than men were previously married (17% versus 9% overall). Only 53% of women junior faculty have at least one child, compared with 70% of men junior faculty. A higher percentage of part-time, tenure-track faculty than of junior faculty overall are observed to have at least one child among both women (71% versus 53%) and men (83% versus 70%) junior faculty.

### Relationship Between Family Responsibilities and Employment Status Controlling for Other Variables

Table 2 shows the odds-ratios for full-time, nontenure-track employment and part-time, nontenure-track employment relative to full-time, tenure-track employment among junior faculty. Columns 1 and 2 represent the "baseline" model that includes only measures of sex and race. Columns 3 and 4 show the relationship between family responsibilities and employment status controlling for differences in sex and race. Columns 5 and 6 show the odds-ratios when human capital characteristics are added to the model, and columns 7 and 8 show the odds-ratios when structural characteristics are also taken into account. The likelihood ratio test indicating the probability that all of the variables in the model are jointly equal to zero is rejected at the 0.1% level for all specifications.

The multinomial logistic regression analyses reveal that, controlling only for race, women are more likely to hold both full-time and part-time, nontenure-track positions than full-time, tenure-track positions (columns 1 & 2). Adding controls for family responsibilities does not change the relationship between sex and employment status (columns 3 & 4). Adding measures of human capital to the model eliminates the statistically significant relationship between sex and the likelihood of holding a part-time, nontenure-track position rather than a full-time, tenure-track position (column 6). Even after controlling for differences in race, family responsibilities, human capital, and structural characteristics, however, the odds of holding a full-time, nontenure-track position rather than a full-time, tenure-track position are higher for women than for men. These findings suggest that differences in race, family responsibilities, human capital, and structural characteristics do not fully account for the observed higher representation of women in full-time, nontenure-track positions.

Married faculty and previously married faculty are more likely than never married faculty to hold part-time, nontenure-track positions than full-time, tenure-track positions after controlling only for sex and race (column 4). Controlling also for human capital investment, however, eliminates these relationships (column 6). Contrary to expectations

TABLE 2

Odds-Ratios for Employment Status of Junior Faculty

| Independent Variable | Sex and Race | | Family Responsibilities | | Human Capital | | Structural Characteristics | |
|---|---|---|---|---|---|---|---|---|
| | 1 Full-time, Nontenure Track | 2 Part-time, Nontenure Track | 3 Full-time, Nontenure Track | 4 Part-time, Nontenure Track | 5 Full-time, Nontenure Track | 6 Part-time, Nontenure Track | 7 Full-time, Nontenure Track | 8 Part-time, Nontenure Track |
| Female | 1.45*** | 1.15* | 1.43*** | 1.15* | 1.31** | 1.03 | 1.32** | 1.02 |
| Black | 0.97 | 0.65*** | 0.98 | 0.66*** | 0.91 | 0.63*** | 0.90 | 0.61*** |
| Hispanic | 0.69 | 0.82 | 0.70 | 0.83 | 0.62* | 0.74 | 0.66 | 0.59** |
| Asian | 0.74 | 0.54*** | 0.75 | 0.54*** | 1.07 | 1.06 | 0.97 | 1.08 |
| Married | | | 1.01 | 1.31** | 0.95 | 1.11 | 1.00 | 1.08 |
| Previously married | | | 0.93 | 1.36** | 0.87 | 1.04 | 0.96 | 0.95 |
| At least one child | | | 0.89 | 0.95 | 0.81** | 0.76*** | 0.79** | 0.83* |
| Less than doctorate | | | | | 3.38*** | 6.35*** | 4.29*** | 6.29*** |
| PhD from non-Research I | | | | | 1.05 | 1.61*** | 1.11 | 1.57*** |
| Research assistantship | | | | | 0.78** | 0.70*** | 0.75** | 0.73*** |
| Teaching assistantship | | | | | 1.08 | 0.72** | 1.07 | 0.67*** |
| Years since highest degree | | | | | 1.03*** | 1.05*** | 1.02*** | 1.05*** |
| Years in current position | | | | | 1.06*** | 1.05*** | 1.05*** | 1.06*** |
| Only job since highest degree | | | | | 1.24* | 0.27*** | 1.12 | 0.27*** |
| Other doctoral | | | | | | | 0.69** | 0.47*** |
| Comprehensive I | | | | | | | 0.65*** | 0.66*** |
| Other 4-year | | | | | | | 0.57*** | 0.48*** |
| Specialized | | | | | | | 0.24*** | 1.02 |
| Two-year | | | | | | | 0.69 | 0.71* |
| Unionized institution | | | | | | | 1.15 | 1.07 |
| Nursing & other health | | | | | | | 1.16 | 0.65* |
| English & foreign languages | | | | | | | 1.75** | 2.11*** |
| Education | | | | | | | 1.24 | 1.57*** |

TABLE 2 (*Continued*)

| Independent Variable | Sex and Race | | Family Responsibilities | | Human Capital | | Structural Characteristics | |
|---|---|---|---|---|---|---|---|---|
| | 1 Full-time, Nontenure Track | 2 Part-time, Nontenure Track | 3 Full-time, Nontenure Track | 4 Part-time, Nontenure Track | 5 Full-time, Nontenure Track | 6 Part-time, Nontenure Track | 7 Full-time, Nontenure Track | 8 Part-time, Nontenure Track |
| Fine arts | | | | | | | 0.68 | 1.46* |
| Psychology, sociology, other | | | | | | | 1.36 | 2.57*** |
| Other field | | | | | | | 1.08 | 1.16 |
| Biology | | | | | | | 0.90 | 1.14 |
| Mathematics & computer sci | | | | | | | 1.74* | 1.30 |
| Business | | | | | | | 1.27 | 1.06 |
| Econ., pol. sci., history, law, philosophy | | | | | | | 1.14 | 1.38 |
| First-professional health | | | | | | | 1.76* | 0.98 |
| Number of cases in analyses | 6,270 | | 6,270 | | 6,270 | | 6,270 | |
| $X^2$, *df* (change −2 log likelihood) | 66, | 8*** | 83, | 14*** | 1,900, | 28*** | 2,360, | 62*** |
| Pseudo $R^2$ (Cox & Snell) | 0.01 | | 0.01 | | 0.26 | | 0.31 | |
| Percent classified correctly | 0.49 | | 0.49 | | 0.65 | | 0.66 | |

Source: Analyses of 1993 National Study of Postsecondary Faculty (NSOPF:93).
Notes: Employment status is relative to full-time, tenure-track employment. Institutional type is relative to Research I university. Academic field is relative to engineering and physical science.
***$p < 0.001$.   **$p < 0.01$.   *$p < 0.05$.

based on human capital theory, junior faculty with at least one child are marginally ($p < 0.05$) less likely to hold both full-time and part-time, nontenure-track positions than full-time, tenure-track positions even after controlling for differences in other variables.

The analyses also reveal that educational attainment is an important predictor of employment status. The odds of holding either a full-time or part-time, nontenure-track position rather than a full-time, tenure-track position are substantially higher for faculty who have not earned a doctorate even after taking other differences into account. Holding a research assistantship during graduate school reduces the odds of holding either a full-time or part-time, nontenure-track position, net of other variables, while holding a teaching assistantship reduces the odds of holding a part-time, nontenure-track position. Junior faculty at non-Research I four-year colleges and universities appear to be less likely than junior faculty at Research I universities to hold full-time or part-time, nontenure-track positions. The odds of holding a part-time, nontenure-track position appear to be higher for faculty working in fields with among the highest proportions of women, English and foreign languages, education, fine arts, and psychology, sociology, and other social sciences. In contrast, faculty in the category with the highest proportion of women, nursing and non-first professional health, appear to be less likely to hold part-time, nontenure-track positions. These findings suggest that the concentration of women in particular academic fields may be related to the segregation of women by employment status.

To more fully explore sex differences in the relationship between family responsibilities and employment status, the analyses are repeated for women and men separately. The results, summarized in Table 3, show that, consistent with human capital theory, the odds of holding a part-time, nontenure-track position appear to be higher for married women than for other women even after controlling for race, human capital investment, and structural characteristics. Marital status appears to be unrelated to employment status among men junior faculty. Whereas having at least one child is unrelated to employment status for women junior faculty after controlling for other variables, men who have at least one child appear to be less likely than their childless male counterparts to hold a full-time, nontenure-track position.

### *Satisfaction with Nontenure-Track Employment Among Junior Faculty*

Anecdotal evidence suggests that some fraction of nontenure-track faculty are content with their employment status because they prefer to spend their time on other well-paying jobs, hobbies, or raising children

TABLE 3

Odds-Ratios for Employment Status of Women and Men Junior Faculty: Fall 1992

| Independent Variable | Full-time, Nontenure Track Women | Men | Part-time, Nontenure Track Women | Men |
|---|---|---|---|---|
| Black | 0.81 | 1.01 | 0.45*** | 0.78 |
| Hispanic | 0.48 | 0.79 | 0.84 | 0.45*** |
| Asian | 1.17 | 0.95 | 1.19 | 1.00 |
| Married | 1.09 | 0.95 | 1.41* | 0.78 |
| Previously married | 0.85 | 1.11 | 1.10 | 0.84 |
| At least one child | 0.99 | 0.62** | 0.90 | 0.82 |
| Less than doctorate | 4.12*** | 4.44*** | 8.34*** | 5.29*** |
| PhD from non-Research I | 1.42 | 0.91 | 2.09*** | 1.29 |
| Research assistantship | 0.64** | 0.84 | 0.65** | 0.82 |
| Teaching assistantship | 1.10 | 1.05 | 0.63*** | 0.68*** |
| Number of years since highest degree | 1.00 | 1.04*** | 1.04*** | 1.06*** |
| Number of years in current position | 1.08*** | 1.04** | 1.05*** | 1.06*** |
| Only job since highest degree | 0.84 | 1.42* | 0.31*** | 0.21*** |
| Unionized institution | 0.97 | 1.31* | 0.88 | 1.29** |
| Other doctoral | 0.55** | 0.89 | 0.45*** | 0.53*** |
| Comprehensive I | 0.43*** | 0.98 | 0.61** | 0.73* |
| Other 4-year | 0.31*** | 1.08 | 0.40*** | 0.58** |
| Two-year | 0.14*** | 0.45** | 0.85 | 1.33 |
| Specialized institution | 0.50* | 0.92 | 0.94 | 0.61* |
| Nursing & other health | 1.30 | 0.93 | 0.68 | 1.03 |
| English & foreign languages | 2.04 | 1.79* | 3.07** | 1.62* |
| Education | 1.26 | 1.52 | 2.29* | 1.21 |
| Fine arts | 1.02 | 0.48* | 2.39* | 1.15 |
| Psychology, sociology, other | 1.57 | 1.34 | 3.60*** | 2.29*** |
| Other field | 1.03 | 1.14 | 1.18 | 1.30 |
| Biology | 1.13 | 0.80 | 1.69 | 1.00 |
| Mathematics & computer science | 1.91 | 1.76* | 1.24 | 1.49 |
| Business | 1.52 | 0.83 | 1.29 | 1.21 |
| Econ., pol. sci., history, law, philosophy | 1.55 | 0.93 | 1.84 | 1.28 |
| First-professional health | 1.56 | 2.00* | 0.89 | 1.12 |
| Number of cases in the analyses | 2,902 | 3,368 | | |
| $R^2$, *df* (change -2 log likelihood) | 1,081, 60*** | 1,407, 60*** | | |
| Pseudo $R^2$ (Cox & Snell) | 0.311 | 0.341 | | |
| Percent classified correctly | 66% | 68% | | |

SOURCE: Analyses of 1993 National Study of Postsecondary Faculty (NSOPF:93).
NOTES: Employment status is relative to full-time, tenure-track employment. Institutional type is relative to Research I university. Academic field is relative to engineering and physical science.
***$p < 0.001$.    **$p < 0.01$.    *$p < 0.05$.

(Flynn, Flynn, Grimm & Lockhart, 1986; Wilson, 1998). Exploring the extent to which junior faculty are satisfied holding part-time and non-tenure-track positions is limited by the variables available in the NSOPF:93 database. For example, part-time faculty, but not full-time, nontenure-track faculty, were asked their reasons for their current employment status. Descriptive analyses of the available data reveal that women and men are equally likely to report holding part-time, non-tenure-track positions because they prefer to work part-time (about 56%). Table 4 shows that women are more likely than men to report holding a part-time, nontenure-track position because a full-time position is unavailable (49% versus 38%) but less likely to report holding a part-time, nontenure-track position because they are supplementing their incomes (48% versus 61%). These data suggest that, despite a generally stated preference for working part-time, women may actually be less likely than men to hold part-time, nontenure-track positions because they have voluntarily chosen such status.

Another approach to understanding the extent to which junior faculty are satisfied holding nontenure-track positions is to examine the relative importance of various characteristics in a decision to leave the current job. The descriptive data presented in Table 5 suggest that, among both women and men, the prospect of a tenured position is somewhat less important for faculty holding nontenure-track positions than for faculty holding full-time, tenure-track positions (about 47% versus 64%). Opportunity for advancement and job security are very important for most faculty, although both appear to be somewhat less important for part-time, nontenure-track faculty than for full-time, tenure-track faculty. Despite these differences, the data suggest that a substantial portion of women and men nontenure-track faculty are interested in a tenured position, opportunity for advancement, and job security. The importance of some characteristics that are likely associated with family responsibilities, such as geographic location and schools for children, does not appear to vary by employment status. Among both women and men, the

TABLE 4

Reasons Part-time, Nontenure-Track Faculty Are Working Part-time: Fall 1992

| Characteristic | Total | Women | Men | Statistical Difference |
|---|---|---|---|---|
| Total | 100% | 100% | 100% | |
| Preferred part-time | 56% | 55% | 57% | n.s. |
| Full-time unavailable | 43% | 49% | 38% | *** |
| Supplementing income | 55% | 48% | 61% | *** |
| To be in academic environment | 71% | 71% | 71% | n.s. |
| Finishing graduate degree | 9% | 11% | 7% | *** |
| Other reason | 20% | 20% | 20% | n.s. |

SOURCE: Analyses of 1993 National Study of Postsecondary Faculty (NSOPF:93).
NOTE: n.s. indicates not statistically significant.
***$p < 0.001$.    **$p < 0.01$.    *$p < 0.05$.

availability of a job for the spouse appears to be somewhat less important for part-time, nontenure-track faculty than for full-time faculty. Regardless of employment status, however, spousal employment appears to be a more important concern for women than for men. Nonetheless, both women and men junior faculty appear to be satisfied with their choice of profession regardless of employment status. Table 6 shows that, on average, both women and men junior faculty generally agree that they would choose an academic career again.

## Conclusions and Implications

Although Bowen and Schuster (1986) predicted that differences in the status of, and rewards received by, women and men faculty would diminish as the number of women entering academic careers continued to increase, the findings from this study show that sex differences continue to exist in employment status. Even after controlling for differences in race, family responsibilities, human capital, and structural characteristics, women are more likely than men to hold full-time, nontenure positions, positions of lower status in the academic labor market hierarchy.

TABLE 5

Percent of Junior Faculty Reporting Various Characteristics to be Very Important in the Decision to Leave Current Job: Fall 1992

| Characteristic | Sex | Total | Full-time, Tenure Track | Full-time, Nontenure Track | Part-time, Nontenure Track |
|---|---|---|---|---|---|
| Tenured position | Total | 51% | 64% | 47% | 42% |
| | Women | 52% | 65% | 48% | 44% |
| | Men | 50% | 64% | 46% | 40% |
| Opportunity advancement | Total | 61% | 66% | 62% | 57% |
| | Women | 63% | 69% | 65% | 59% |
| | Men | 59% | 64% | 59% | 55% |
| Job security | Total | 68% | 74% | 72% | 63% |
| | Women | 72% | 76% | 77% | 69% |
| | Men | 64% | 72% | 66% | 57% |
| Geographic location | Total | 59% | 61% | 58% | 58% |
| | Women | 61% | 63% | 60% | 61% |
| | Men | 58% | 60% | 56% | 55% |
| Schools for children | Total | 54% | 58% | 53% | 52% |
| | Women | 53% | 53% | 54% | 52% |
| | Men | 55% | 62% | 52% | 51% |
| Job for spouse | Total | 44% | 51% | 48% | 37% |
| | Women | 49% | 56% | 57% | 42% |
| | Men | 39% | 48% | 39% | 33% |

SOURCE: Analyses of 1993 National Study of Postsecondary Faculty (NSOPF:93).

TABLE 6

Level of Agreement that a Junior Faculty Member Would Choose an Academic Career Again: Fall 1992

| Sex | Total | Full-time, Tenure Track | Full-time, Nontenure Track | Part-time, Nontenure Track |
|---|---|---|---|---|
| Women | 3.43 | 3.45 | 3.40 | 3.40 |
| Men | 3.45 | 3.46 | 3.42 | 3.45 |

SOURCE: Analyses of 1993 National Study of Postsecondary Faculty (NSOPF:93).
NOTE: Scale is from 1 to 4, with 1 indicating strongly disagree and 4 indicating strongly agree.

Though both human capital and structural approaches were shown to be useful for understanding the distribution of faculty by employment status, the results of this research suggest that human capital and structural approaches to the academic labor market do not fully account for the concentration of women in full-time, nontenure-track positions. One possible explanation for this finding is that the model omitted, or inadequately measured, important aspects of human capital and structural characteristics, as described in the limitations section. A second possible explanation is that women prefer to hold full-time, nontenure-track positions for reasons that are not adequately captured by the available proxies for family responsibilities. The finding that about 55% of women with part-time, nontenure-track appointments prefer to work part-time may be consistent with this explanation. Alternatively, women may be more likely to hold these lower status positions because they are perceived by colleges and universities to be less productive and/or incapable of succeeding in full-time, tenure-track positions. The descriptive data showing that a higher share of women than men are working part-time because a full-time position is unavailable may support the appropriateness of this explanation.

The findings from this study also suggest that the employment of women in nontenure-track positions is attributable in part to their marital and parental status. Although a smaller share of women than men junior faculty are married (67% versus 78%), being married increases the odds of holding a part-time, nontenure-track position for women but not for men. While a smaller share of women than men junior faculty have at least one child (53% versus 70%), having at least one child reduces the odds of holding a full-time, nontenure-track position for men but is unrelated to employment status for women. As Toutkoushian (1998) noted, these sex differences in employment status for women and men faculty may be attributable to either differences in the supply of women and men faculty who are married or parents or to differences in the demand for faculty who are married or parents. Regardless, while some research (e.g., Bellas, 1992; Toutkoushian, 1998) has shown that married men faculty benefit from having wives in terms of their productivity and salaries, this study suggests that married men faculty and men faculty with children are also benefiting from their marital and parental status in terms of their employment status.

Because the NSOPF:93 lacks variables describing the nature of the spouse's employment, future research should examine the extent to which married women are more likely to hold part-time, nontenure-track positions because they are married to other academics. Using a national survey of college and university faculty in 1989, Astin and Milem (1997) showed that a higher share of married women faculty than married men faculty are married to other academics (40% versus 35%). Whereas some research suggests that women with academic spouses may be benefitting in terms of their productivity, rank, and salaries possibly because of greater access to collegial networks (Astin & Milem, 1997), this study suggests that married women—a substantial proportion of whom are likely to have academic spouses—may be disadvantaged with regard to their employment status because of a lack of mobility.

On the surface, the descriptive analyses suggest that a substantial portion of women and men junior faculty are relatively satisfied holding lower status (i.e., nontenure-track) positions. Regardless of employment status, both women and men generally agreed that they would choose an academic career again. Nonetheless, future research should also further explore the satisfaction of women and men nontenure-track faculty, particularly given the conclusion of Tack and Patitu (1992) that many married women faculty may be "diluting their professional ambitions and assuming part-time faculty positions" because the demands of work and family are too overwhelming (p. 53).

To some extent, the participation of women in the labor force may always be limited by family responsibilities (Hough, 1987). Even though the share of men who are assuming care-giving responsibilities is growing (Bond et al., 1997), the effects of marital and parental responsibilities on faculty careers are likely to continue to be greater for women than men (Gappa & Leslie, 1993). Dual career relationships typically require one or both partners to make sacrifices regarding career opportunities, particularly in terms of where to live (Gappa & Leslie, 1993). Marriage is likely to impose a greater hardship on the career development and advancement of women than men because a higher percentage of employed women than of employed men are in dual career marriages (89% versus 69%) (Bond et al., 1997). Moreover, even in the 1990s, many families may focus on maximizing the husband's rather than the wife's employment status (Marwell et al., 1979). McElrath (1992) found that, among criminology faculty, women were three times as likely to interrupt their careers because of reasons related to their husband's employment than for maternity. After controlling for education, experience, publications, and parental status, a career disruption and the number of job changes were associated with a lower probability of tenure for women and, among tenured women, a longer time to tenure. In contrast, career disruptions and job changes were unrelated to either the probability of being tenured or the number of years to tenure among men (McElrath, 1992). The findings from this study further suggest that the effects of family responsibilities are less advantageous for women than for men.

Some critics of human capital theory have argued that "many workers who could contribute to the economic advance of the nation have been confined to low-status jobs where they are not allowed to be productive" (DeYoung, 1989, p. 161). Because of the challenges Youn (1992) identifies with moving across segments of the academic labor market, faculty who hold nontenure-track appointments but who aspire to tenure-track or tenured appointments are unlikely to achieve their goal. A number of researchers (e.g., Bowen & Schuster, 1986; Chronister, Baldwin & Bailey, 1996; Franklin, Laurence, & Denham, 1988; Gappa & Leslie, 1993; Kasper, Bronner, Gray, Kreiser, & Rosenthal, 1986; Lomperis, 1990; Rajagopal & Farr, 1992;) have concluded that part-time and nontenure-track faculty generally receive less encouragement and support for research activities, as evidenced by their less desirable teaching assignments and heavier teaching loads, lack of collegial support, and lack of access to resources for research including release time, funding, and facilities.

From an institutional perspective, the use of nontenure-track faculty may appear to have some financial and programmatic advantages. Nontenure-track appointments may provide colleges and universities with greater flexibility to respond to enrollment changes and shifts in enrollment across academic disciplines and may enable them to offer specialized courses without the commitment of resources that a tenure-track appointment entails. Nonetheless, Kasper et al. (1986), Franklin et al. (1988), and others have argued that the increasing use of part-time and nontenure-track faculty undermines academic standards and diminishes the quality of undergraduate education. Gappa and Leslie (1993) concluded, based on their examination of the use of part-time faculty at 18 colleges and universities, that using part-time faculty does not necessarily improve efficiency or cost effectiveness. As an example, the use of part-time and nontenure-track faculty typically requires that tenured and tenure track full-time faculty assume the burden of student advising, committee work, and other activities in which nontenure-track faculty do not fully participate.

Although some (e.g., Franklin et al., 1988) have recommended that some nontenure-track positions be converted to tenure-track assistant professor appointments, nontenure-track faculty are likely to continue to comprise a substantial proportion of our nation's faculty (Gappa & Leslie, 1993). The findings from this research suggest that individual colleges and universities should reexamine their policies and procedures regarding recruitment and tenure. With regard to recruitment, institutions should ensure that the tendency of women to hold full-time, nontenure-track positions rather than full-time, tenure-track positions is attributable to a genuine preference for such positions. Colleges and universities should also examine their policies and procedures regarding tenure to ensure that women are not pressured to choose between a tenure-track position and motherhood. This study showed that only 2% of junior faculty nationwide hold part-time, tenure-track positions. Of 191 colleges and universities in one survey, only 11% had a policy offering tenure to part-time faculty (Raabe, 1997). By creating flexibility in the tenure process (e.g., by allowing part-time faculty to pursue tenure), and by ensuring that all administrators and faculty understand the need for such policies (Finkel et al., 1994), colleges and universities will help to establish a more "family friendly" environment.

As others (e.g., Marshall & Jones, 1990; Sorcinelli & Near, 1989) have suggested, all faculty would benefit from institutional efforts that support faculty in managing work and family roles. The Families and Work Institute concluded from its 1997 survey of employees in a variety of occupations nationwide that a supportive workplace environment is critical to the effectiveness, satisfaction, commitment, and retention of workers regardless of industry (Bond et al., 1997). A study of faculty at one university suggests that job and life satisfaction are more highly correlated among college and university faculty than among the general population (Sorcinelli & Near, 1989). Both married men and women with children are concerned about dual careers, commuter marriages, and childrearing (Sorcinelli & Near, 1989). Therefore, all faculty would likely benefit from such initiatives as workshops on time and stress management and sex role socialization, supportive counseling (especially during family and career changes), higher quality and more available childcare, and employment assistance for spouses and partners, as well as more flexible leaves and sabbaticals. Nonetheless, a 1991 survey of 191 colleges and universities showed that, while most institutions had a policy regarding unpaid or paid leave for mothers at childbirth, less than one-half had policies covering job assistance for the spouse, accommodative scheduling, unpaid leave for fathers at childbirth, or on-campus childcare centers (Raabe, 1997). Moreover, even when such policies as accommodative scheduling and job sharing are in place, they are reported to be only rarely used (Raabe, 1997). By adopting and encouraging the use of policies, practices, and initiatives that recognize that many faculty are also spouses and parents, colleges and universities will create an environment that fosters the success of both women and men faculty.

## References

Astin, H. S., & Bayer, A. E. (1979). Pervasive sex differences in the academic reward system. In D. R. Lewis & W. E. Becker (Eds.), *Academic Rewards in Higher Education* (Chap. 10). Cambridge, MA: Balinger.

Astin, H. S., & Davis, D. E. (1985). Research productivity across the life and career cycles: Facilitators and barriers for women. In M. F. Fox (Ed.), *Scholarly writing and publishing: Issues, problems, and solutions.* Boulder, CO: Westview Press.

Astin, H. S., & Milem, J. F. (1997). The status of academic couples in U.S. institutions. In M. A. Ferber & J. W. Loeb (Eds.), *Academic couples: Problems and Promises* (pp. 128–155). Urbana: University of Illinois Press.

Austin, A. E., & Pilat, M. (1990). Tension, stress, and the tapestry of faculty lives. *Academe, 77,* 38–42.

Barbezat, D. (1988). Gender differences in the academic reward system. In D. W. Breneman & T. I. Youn (Eds.), *Academic labor markets and careers* (pp. 138–164). New York: The Falmer Press.

Becker, G. S. (1962). Investment in human capital: A theoretical analysis. *Journal of Political Economy, 70 Supplement* (5), 9–49.

Becker, G. S. (1985). Human capital, effort, and the sexual division of labor. *Journal of Labor Economics, 3*(1), S33–S58.

Becker, G. S. (1993). *Human capital.* Chicago: University of Chicago Press.

Bellas, M. L. (1992). The effects of marital status and wives' employment on the salaries of faculty men: The (house) wife bonus. *Gender & Society, 6,* 609–622.

Bellas, M. L. (1994). Comparable worth in academia: The effects on faculty salaries of the sex composition and labor-market conditions of academic disciplines. *American Sociological Review, 59,* 807–821.

Bellas, M. L. (1997a). Disciplinary differences in faculty salaries: Does gender bias play a role? *Journal of Higher Education, 68,* 299–321.

Bellas, M.L. (1997b). The scholarly productivity of academic couples. In M. A. Ferber & J. W. Loeb (Eds.), *Academic couples: Problems and promises.* Urbana: University of Illinois Press.

Bellas, M. L., & Toutkoushian, R. K. (1999). Faculty time allocations and research productivity: Gender, race, and family effects. *Review of Higher Education, 22,* 367–390.

Bielby, D. D., & Bielby, W. T. (1988). She works hard for the money: Household responsibilities and the allocation of work effort. *American Journal of Sociology, 93,* 1031–1059.

Bond, J. T., Galinsky, E., & Swanberg, J. E. (1997). *The 1997 national study of the changing workforce.* New York: Families and Work Institute.

Bowen, H. R., & Schuster, J. H. (1986). *American professors: A national resource imperiled.* New York: Oxford University Press.

Bronstein, P., Rothblum, E. D., & Solomon, S. E. (1993). Ivy halls and glass walls: Barriers to academic careers for women and ethnic minorities. In J. Gainen & R. Boice (Eds.), *Building a diverse faculty* (Vol. 53, pp. 17–31). San Francisco: Jossey-Bass Publishers.

Chronister, J. L., Baldwin, R. G., & Bailey, T. (1996). Full-time non-tenure track faculty: Current status, condition, and attitudes. In D. E. Finnegan, D. Webster, & Z. F. Gamson (Eds.), *Faculty and faculty issues in colleges and universities* (2nd ed., pp. 326–336). Needham Heights, MA: Simon & Schuster Custom Publishing, ASHE Reader Series.

Chronister, J. L., Gansneder, B. M., Harper, E., & Baldwin, R. G. (1997). Full-time non-tenure track faculty. *NEA Higher Education Research Center Update, 3*(5), 1–4.

Cole, J. R., & Zuckerman, H. (1987). Marriage, motherhood, and research performance in science. *Scientific American, 256*(2), 119–125.

Cooney, T. M., & Uhlenberg, P. (1989). Family-building patterns of professional women: A comparison of lawyers, physicians, and postsecondary teachers. *Journal of Marriage and the Family, 51,* 749–758.

Creamer, E. G. (1998). *Assessing faculty publication productivity: Issues of equity.* (ASHE-ERIC Higher Education Report Vol. 26, No. 2). Washington, DC: The George Washington University: Graduate School of Education and Human Development.

Dey, E. L. (1994). Dimensions of faculty stress: A recent survey. *Review of Higher Education, 17,* 305–322.

DeYoung, A. J. (1989). *Economics and American education: A historical and critical overview of the impact of economic theories on schooling in the United States.* White Plains, NY: Longman Inc.

Dreijmanis, J. (1991). Higher education and employment: Is professional employment a right? *Higher Education Review, 23*(3), 7–18.

England, P. (1982). The failure of human capital theory to explain occupational sex segregation. *Journal of Human Resources, 17,* 358–370.

Ferber, M. A., & Hoffman, E. P. (1997). Are academic partners at a disadvantage? In M. A. Ferber & J. W. Loeb (Eds.), *Academic couples: Problems and promises.* Urbana: University of Illinois Press.

Finkel, S. K., Olswang, S., & She, N. (1994). Childbirth, tenure, and promotion for women faculty. *Review of Higher Education, 17,* 259–270.

Flynn, E. A., Flynn, J. F., Grimm, N., & Lockhart, T. (1986). The part-time problem: Four voices. *Academe, 72*(1), 12–18.

Franklin, P., Laurence, D., & Denham, R. D. (1988). When solutions become problems: Taking a stand on part-time employment. *Academe, 74*(3), 15–19.

Gappa, J., & Leslie, D. (1993). *The invisible faculty: Improving the status of part-timers in higher education.* San Francisco: Jossey-Bass.

Hamovitch, W., & Morgenstern, R. D. (1977). Children and the productivity of academic women. *Journal of Higher Education, 48,* 633–645.

Hough, J. R. (1987). *Education and the national economy.* New York: Croom Helm.

Johnson, G. E., & Stafford, F. P. (1974). The earnings and promotion of women faculty. *American Economic Review, 64,* 888–903.

Kasper, H., Bronner, F., Gray, M. W., Kreiser, B. R., & Rosenthal, J. R. (1986). 1986 report on full-time non-tenure track appointments. *Academe, 72*(4), 14a-19a.

Kasten, K. L. (1984). Tenure and merit pay as rewards for research, teaching, and service at a research university. *Journal of Higher Education, 55,* 500–514.

Kirshstein, R. J., Matheson, N., & Jing, Z. (1997). *Instructional faculty and staff in higher education institutions: Fall 1987 and Fall 1992.* Washington, DC: U.S. Department of Education, National Center for Education Statistics (NCES 97–447).

Korenman, S., & Neumark, D. (1991). Marriage, motherhood, and wages. *Journal of Human Resources, 27,* 233–255.

Lomperis, A. M. T. (1990). Are women changing the nature of the academic profession? *Journal of Higher Education, 61,* 643–677.

Marshall, M. R., & Jones, C. H. (1990). Childbearing sequence and the career development of women administrators in higher education. *Journal of College Student Development, 31,* 531–537.

Marwell, G., Rosenfeld, R., & Spilerman, S. (1979). Geographic constraints on women's career in academia. *Science, 205,* 1225–1231.

McElrath, K. (1992). Gender, career disruption, and academic rewards. *Journal of Higher Education, 63,* 269–281.

Menard, S. (1995). *Applied logistic regression analysis.* Thousand Oaks: Sage.

Polachek, S. W. (1977). Occupational segregation among women: Theory, evidence, and a prognosis. In C. B. Lloyd, E. S. Andrews, & C. L. Gilroy (Eds.), *Women in the Labor Market.* New York: Columbia University Press.

Raabe, P. H. (1997). Work-family policies for faculty: How "career- and family-friendly" is academe? In M. A. Ferber & J. W. Loeb (Eds.), *Academic couples: Problems and Promises* (pp. 208–225). Urbana: University of Illinois Press.

Rajagopal, I., & Farr, W. D. (1992). Hidden academics: The part-time faculty in Canada. *Higher Education, 24,* 317–331.

Riemenschnieder, A., & Harper, K. V. (1990). Women in academia: Guilty or not guilty? Conflict between caregiving and employment. *Initiatives, 53*(2), 27–35.

Rosenfeld, R. A., & Jones, J. A. (1987). Patterns and effects of geographic mobility for academic women and men. *Journal of Higher Education, 58,* 493–515.

Smart, J. C. (1991). Gender equity in academic rank and salary. *Review of Higher Education, 14,* 511–526.

Smart, J. C., & McLaughlin, G. W. (1978). Reward structures of academic disciplines. *Research in Higher Education, 8,* 39–55.

Sorcinelli, M. D., & Near, J. P. (1989). Relations between work and life away from work among university faculty. *Journal of Higher Education, 60,* 59–81.

Sorenson, E. (1989). Measuring the effect of occupational sex and race composition on earnings. In R. T. Michael, H. I. Hartmann, & B. O'Farrell (Eds.), *Pay equity: Empirical inquiries* (chap. 2). Washington, DC: National Academy Press.

Tack, M. W., & Patitu, C. L. (1992). *Faculty job satisfaction: Women and minorities in peril.* (ASHE-ERIC Higher Education Report No. 4). Washington, DC: The George Washington University, School of Education and Human Development.

Toutkoushian, R. K. (1998). Racial and marital status differences in faculty pay. *Journal of Higher Education, 69,* 513–541.

Wilson, R. (1998, July). For some adjunct faculty members, the tenure track holds little appeal. *Chronicle of Higher Education,* pp. A9–A10.

Youn, T. I. K. (1988). Studies of academic markets and careers: An historical review. In D. W. Breneman, & T. I. K. Youn (Eds.), *Academic labor markets and careers* (chap. 1, pp. 8–27). New York: The Falmer Press.

Youn, T. I. K. (1992). The sociology of academic careers and academic labor markets. *Research in Labor Markets, 13,* 101–130.

# Review Essay

The Role of Faculty in Assessing Colleagues' Teaching
*The Peer Review of Teaching: A Sourcebook,*
by Nancy Van Note Chism.
Bolton, MA: Anker, 1999. 141 pp., $24.95 (paper)

LARRY KEIG, The University of Northern Iowa

For well over twenty years, peer review of college teaching has been promoted in the exhortative literature, justified in theory, and supported by reports of experimental and qualitative research. Yet, except for the faculty's role in personnel decision making, peer review is rarely practiced; and even when and where it has been put into place (interestingly, mostly at the departmental level of research universities, where results sometimes have been reported in journals), it hardly ever has sustained itself for any appreciable length of time. In *Peer Review of Teaching,* Chism suggests that one reason for its infrequent practice is a lack of guiding principles and materials for developing and implementing it.

Chism compellingly argues for the involvement of faculty in assessing colleagues' teaching and—probably most significantly—provides a wide range of useful materials for peer review of many teaching-related activities. She clearly describes the potential value of peer review for both improving teaching (formative evaluation) and making decisions regarding reappointment, tenure, promotion, and merit compensation (summative evaluation). She also persuasively argues not only for employing it alongside student ratings of courses and instructors but also for other forms of assessment, recognizing that credible efforts to improve and assess teaching require a comprehensiveness not often found

*Larry Keig is assistant professor, Department of Educational Leadership, Counseling, and Postsecondary Education.*

*The Journal of Higher Education,* Vol. 72, No. 5 (September/October 2001)

in college faculty evaluation. She unquestionably provides the best and most extensive collection of tools for the peer review of teaching to date.

The book is in two parts. The four chapters comprising Part 1 provide an overview: Developing a Rationale and Understanding of Peer Review (Chapter 1), Setting Up a System of Peer Review (Chapter 2), Understanding Roles and Goals of a Peer Review System (Chapter 3), and Identifying the Focus of a Peer Review of Teaching System (Chapter 4). Five chapters, which correspond to different methods of peer review, make up Part 2: Peer Review of Course Materials (Chapter 5), Classroom Observation (Chapter 6), Leadership for Teaching: Contributing to Scholarship of Teaching and Departmental Teaching Efforts (Chapter 7), Teaching Portfolios (Chapter 8), and Summary (Chapter 9). Chapters 5 through 9 include the practical "how to" information (resources and forms) that practitioners could use in assessing colleagues' teaching performance; this is what readers who want to know what and how to peer review should find especially useful.

Chism almost certainly would support Centra's contention that "unless faculty members are willing to leave the evaluation of teaching to students, who possess only a limited view, or to administrators, who don't have the time or necessary background, then they must be willing to invest their time in efforts at peer evaluation of teaching" (1986, p. 1). Extending the argument for peer review of teaching further, Chism maintains that it is "the responsibility of the profession to monitor itself, . . . to make teaching 'community property'; . . . that the evaluation of teaching must reflect the complexity of teaching itself; . . . [and] that in order for teaching to be valued, there must be an accepted way to judge it" (p. 6). For the professoriate to take teaching (and, by extension, student learning) seriously, for assessment to reflect teaching's complex nature, and for teaching to be valued as much as research and scholarship (traditionally defined), she insists it must be assessed by multiple sources (peers as well as students and administrators), by a variety of methods (at least evaluation of course materials, leadership for teaching, and teaching portfolios as well as classroom observation), and for at least two different, though complementary purposes (improving teaching as well as making of personnel decisions). She also fairly addresses objections to peer review (e.g., the sanctity of the classroom, the distinctions between peer and colleague, vulnerability of peer reviewers, the time factor, lack of standards of effective teaching and the possible disjunction between "effective teaching" and student learning, validity and reliability issues, and undesirable aftereffects).

In emphasizing resources (i.e., forms for evaluating teaching), Chism may unwittingly promote products more appropriate for summative evaluation than for formative assessment. In saying that the resources in the sourcebook "might be a helpful starting point for the discussion of standards [of effective teaching and that] they should be adapted and modified as the faculty sees fit," (p. 21), however noble the intent, some of the resources she provides may run counter to an approach often recommended for communicating feedback to faculty in improving teaching. Centra has suggested, for example, that for some types of formative peer review qualitative methods may be more valuable than quantitative findings, noting that "a qualitative approach would involve descriptions of classroom instruction based on the perceptions of the observers. Rating scales and numerical judgments would not be necessary or useful. In many instances, in fact, the scales are not appropriate for all styles of teaching. But descriptions by several observers will more likely reflect possible biases and the resulting narrative could be much more useful" (Centra, 1986, pp. 2–3). Even though Chism has suggested, in directions for use on most of the forms, that peer reviewers focus on producing comments, reviewers may be tempted, given time constraints, to rate rather than narrate, to judge rather than describe. Unlike summative review, formative evaluation should include nonjudgmental descriptions of faculty members' teaching, not only by colleagues but also by academic administrators (especially, as Chism perceptively notes, by the department chair) and, where available, teaching consultants.

Chism offers a particularly useful framework for identifying roles faculty should play in assessing peers' teaching: first-order and second-order, noting that both are essential. First-order roles are assessments of "those things that peers are most able to judge [for themselves]." Second-order roles are their reviews of "judgments and evidence submitted by others" (p. 35). In identifying roles in each of these categories, Chism probably relies too heavily on a classification provided by Cohen and McKeachie (1980), good as it is, and not extensively enough on other useful lists and discussions (e.g., Batista, 1976; Scriven, 1980, 1985, 1987; and Soderberg,1986). The roles recommended by all of these scholars (and others) are summarized by Keig and Waggoner (1994, pp. 30–34; 1995, pp. 55–57).

Soderberg's (1986) three-dimensional framework for evaluating college teaching is also useful for thinking about how peer review might contribute to better teaching and more meaningful student learning. According to Soderberg, faculty members' decision making and performance can be assessed by knowledgeable constituencies on their pre-interactive decision making, on how effectively they interact with students, and on how well they "capture the process nature of instruction," including the feedback they and their students receive and act upon (Soderberg, 1986, p. 16). Chism has designed materials for peer reviewers at all three of these stages, focusing primarily on pre-interactive decision making and interaction rather than on, and somewhat at the expense of, process indicators.

Her resources for peer review of course materials, probably best used as guides for narratives on performance and/or conversations between or among faculty, are especially comprehensive and well conceived; in much of this section of the book, she has broken new ground. These resources include assessments of the following: syllabi; ground rules for discussions and other policy and/or procedure documents; course packet and textbook content; course bibliographies; overhead transparencies or presentation slides; course handouts; multimedia course materials; tests written by faculty and administered to students; and class assignments and exercise sheets. They may be less suitable for summative evaluation, where a more global assessment, focusing on a limited number of items, probably is more relevant to those making personnel decisions (McKeachie, 1994, pp. 329–330).

Chism's analysis of the strengths and limitations of classroom observation is probing, and the resources she provides for peer observation capture important elements of interaction between teacher and student. Because peer observation may not be reliable enough to use for summative evaluation (Centra, 1993, 1986; McKeachie, 1994), the resources probably are most suitable for formative peer review. If used for improving teaching, the forms might be best employed as guides for written or verbal non-evaluative feedback of how teachers interact with students. Peer reviewers may find the Narrative Log (pp. 82–84) especially useful because it can "help instructors review a class after it has occurred. They can stimulate recall and freeze the class in time for the purpose of examination . . . [of] the fit of actions to goals, student learning issues, alternative ways situations could have been handled, and the like" (p. 82).

As Cross has noted, "The ultimate criterion of effective teaching is effective learning. There is simply no other reason for teaching. . . . Good teaching is not so much of a performing act as an evocative process. The purpose is to involve students actively in their own learning and to elicit from them their best learning performance (1991, p. 20). In order for students to perform at optimum levels, they need, among other things, to receive meaningful feedback from faculty on their performance. Acknowledging the significance of instructor feedback, Chism has provided a valuable resource for assessing instructor comments on student work, but it regrettably is tucked among the resources for assessing course materials. Because course materials and instructor feedback come at different ends of the teaching process, this resource probably should be one of several in a chapter devoted to peer assessment of faculty evaluation of students' academic work. Although the form Chism provides for assessing instructor comments on student work is generic enough for assessing various types of student work, it seems most appropriate for comments on written assignments. Resources also could be provided for assessing instructor comments on classroom participation, oral communication assignments, cooperative and group learning projects, technology-based projects, student portfolios, inquiry-based projects, experiential learning, and the like. Information provided by chapter authors in Anderson and Speck's 1998 edited book, *Changing the Way We Grade Student Performance: Classroom Assessment and the New Learning Paradigm*, could be used as a springboard for developing additional resources for assessing instructor comments of student work. Chism should not be faulted, though, for not including more resources of this type, because this is largely uncharted territory; however, resources of this type are desperately needed if higher education is to make the shift from the instruction paradigm to the learning paradigm that Barr and Tagg (1995) (and others, in one way or another) have advocated.

In recent years, it has become fashionable to invoke references to *scholarship of teaching* and *teaching portfolios* in discussions of teaching, learning, and assessment. Ernest Boyer's *Scholarship Reconsidered: Priorities of the Professoriate* (1990) has become a tremendously influential, if not fully understood, source in discussions on these issues. College faculty members who consider themselves *teachers* have embraced the premise that professors should be (or become) scholars of teaching because faculty cannot possibly learn everything they need to know about how to teach effectively, and how students learn best and are motivated, from their experiences in classrooms. Yet largely unaddressed (if addressed at all) in discussions on the scholarship of teaching are the means by which professors come to understand the knowledge bases of teaching, learning, and assessment. As in every other scholarly field, the body of literature in each of these areas is extensive but remains largely unknown to most faculty. Using Shulman's broad categories of the knowledge base of teaching as but one example, a teaching scholar would demonstrate *depth* of understanding not only of content in the teaching field but also in general pedagogical knowledge, pedagogical knowledge specific to the content area, curricular knowledge, knowledge of learners, knowledge of educational contexts, and "knowledge of educational ends, purposes, and values, and their philosophical and historical grounds" (Shulman, 1987, p. 8).

Chism's description of the scholarship of teaching—"the activities through which faculty explore conceptions central to the teaching of their field, assess the effects of different teaching strategies on student learning in the discipline, and pose new directions for exploration" (p. 100)—captures the essence of the scholarship of teaching. But her discussion of and resources for the peer review of it appear somewhat superficial, mainly because they are not tied closely enough to the knowledge bases of effective teaching, student learning and motivation, and assessment. (Criticism of this type could also be leveled against most of what has been written on assessing the scholarship of teaching, for the same reasons.) In this same chapter, Chism includes resources for teaching leadership efforts and for nonclassroom teaching activities. These resources are presented in the form of thoughtful questions which could lead to meaningful dialogue among faculty on significant teaching and learning issues and for a peer reviewer's written analyses of another's performance.

In a teaching portfolio, faculty have opportunities to document their teaching philosophy, what and how they teach, the instructional materials they design and use, their students' work along with their comments on and evaluation of it, and how their efforts have been received by students, colleagues, and administrators. In addition, as Chism astutely notes, "A good portfolio is woven together by narrative commentary from the faculty member that describes the context for the documentation and presents reflections on the teaching self. It presents multiple sources of evidence, chronicles the development of the instructor, and projects a future vision" (p. 108). She provides sound information not only on what should be included in a portfolio but also on how it might be peer reviewed. Peer reviewers should find both the insightful questions she lays out for formative assessment and the solid, more global items she includes for summative evaluation useful.

*Teaching* portfolios have been a topic of discussion for improving and evaluating teaching since the 1980s. Discussion on how *course* portfolios might be used for the same purposes has begun more recently. Even though Chism states that "teaching portfolios can concentrate on only one course [as well as] span much longer time periods" (p. 108), it is somewhat surprising she has not integrated the literature on course portfolios with that on teaching portfolios, especially because, as Shulman has pointed out, "The course portfolio is a central element in the argument that teaching and scholarship are neither antithetical nor incompatible, . . . [and that a course], in its design, enactment, and analysis, is as much an act of inquiry and invention as any other activity more traditionally called 'research.'" (1999, p. 5). Chism's argument for a scholarship of teaching probably would be strengthened if she probed what is known about course, as well as teaching, portfolios.

*The Peer Review of Teaching* is not only a valuable addition to the literature on assessment and evaluation but also a significant resource for practitioners looking for more powerful means for reviewing teaching and for improving the quality of student learning. It clearly goes beyond a rehash of exhortative and theoretical literature and research studies. In this book, Chism provides the best materials currently available for assessing course materials and valuable resources for peer classroom observation. It may not include everything that might be desirable: it includes only minimal discussion of and a single resource for peer review of faculty assessment of their students' work, too little on peer review of teaching as scholarly activity, and limited links between teaching and course portfolios as vehicles documenting scholarship of teaching. But she either has introduced or gone well beyond what others have contributed in these areas. Chism herself and others, no doubt, will further the discussion of these topics and contribute even more powerful resources in the future. This book deserves thoughtful reading and consideration by faculty and administrators, and the resources in it should prove valuable as peer review of teaching becomes more commonplace at colleges and universities.

## References

Anderson, R. S., & Speck, B. W. (1998, Summer). *Changing the way we grade student performance: Classroom assessment and the new learning paradigm.* New Directions for Teaching and Learning No. 74. San Francisco: Jossey-Bass.

Barr, R. B., & Tagg, J. (1995, November/December). From teaching to learning—A new paradigm for undergraduate education. *Change,* 13–24.

Batista, E. E. (1976). The place of colleague evaluation in the appraisal of college teaching: A review of the literature. *Research in Higher Education, 4,* 257–271.

Boyer, E. L. (1990). *Scholarship reconsidered: Priorities of the professoriate.* Princeton, NJ: Carnegie Foundation for the Advancement of Teaching.

Centra, J. A. (1986, April). *Colleague evaluation: The critical link.* Paper presented at the annual meeting of the American Educational Research Association, San Francisco, CA. (ERIC Documentation Reproduction Service No. 275 722)

Centra, J. A. (1993). *Reflective faculty evaluation: Enhancing teaching and determining faculty effectiveness.* San Francisco: Jossey-Bass.

Cohen, P. A., & McKeachie, W. J. (1980). The role of colleagues in the evaluation of college teaching. *Improving college and university teaching, 28*(4), 147–154.

Cross, K. P. (1991, Fall). College teaching: What do we know about it? *Innovative Higher Education, 16*(1), 7–25.

Keig, L., & Waggoner, M. D. (1994). *Collaborative peer review: The role of faculty in improving college teaching.* ASHE-ERIC Higher Education Report No. 2. Washington, DC: The George Washington University, School of Education and Human Development.

Keig, L. W., & Waggoner, M. D. (1995). Peer review of teaching: Improving college instruction through formative assessment. *Journal on Excellence in College Teaching,* *6*(3), 51–93.

McKeachie, W. J. (1994). *Teaching tips: Strategies, research, and theory for college and university teachers* (9th ed.). Lexington, MA: Heath.

Scriven, M. S. (1980). *The evaluation of college teaching.* Syracuse, NY: National Council of States on Inservice Education. (ERIC Document Reproduction Service No. 203 729)

Scriven, M. S. (1985). New frontiers of evaluation. *Evaluation Practices, 7*(1), 7–44.

Scriven, M. S. (1987). Validity in personnel evaluation. *Journal of Personnel Evaluation in Education, 1*, 9–23.

Shulman, L. S. (1987). Knowledge and teaching: Foundations of the new reform. *Harvard Educational Review, 57*(1), 1–22.

Shulman, L. S. (1999). Course anatomy: The dissemination and analysis of knowledge through teaching. In P. Hutchings (Ed.), *The course portfolio: How faculty can examine their teaching to* advance *practice and improve student learning* (pp. 5–12). Washington, DC: American Association for Higher Education.

Soderberg, L. O. (1986, March). A credible model: Evaluating classroom teaching in higher education. *Instructional Evaluation, 8*, 13–27.

# Book Reviews

*Enhancing Student Learning: Setting the Campus Context, edited*
by Frances K. Stage, Lemuel W. Watson, and Melvin Terrell.
University Press of America, 1999. 145 pp. $24.00 (paper).

PETER M. MAGOLDA, Miami University

Stage, Watson, and Terrell's primary aim in *Enhancing Student Learning* is to encourage the higher education community—in particular student affairs—to refocus its attention on student learning. In this eight-chapter book, the editors and six additional contributors first make the case that student learning is important, citing numerous instrumental benefits. Next they introduce relevant theories and then provide case studies that demonstrate how these theories could be applied to many higher education settings. The book concludes with a chapter that provides a primer for assessing student learning and a chapter that synthesizes the contributors' main points and speculates on the future. In short, this book is chock-full of reminders and helpful hints that would advance the authors' aim of enhancing student learning. The book does not target readers who desire ground-breaking theoretical perspectives based on original research.

Watson and Stage's introductory chapter encourages readers to think holistically when exploring the complex terrain of student learning. Watson's conceptual model of learning, involvement, and gains is the theoretical framework introduced to accomplish this aim. The model posits that one must concurrently focus on input (e.g., influences of secondary education) process (e.g., the collegiate environment), and output (e.g., educational gains) to influence student learning. Collectively, the model and the case study that follows remind readers of a seldom-contested assertion in student affairs—student learning is shaped by many factors, some of which extend beyond the scope of the classroom (i.e., the traditional venue for "learning").

The "Theories of Learning for College Students" chapter written by Frances Stage and Patricia Muller begins by discussing the usefulness and importance of theory. An eclectic array of theories—self-efficacy, constructivist learning, multiple intelligences, learning styles, and conscientization—follow. These diverse theoretical overviews (i.e., that favor breadth rather than depth) and the accompanying case study examples target student affairs professionals and their work contexts.

Watson and Terrell in their "Cultural Differences in Student Learning and Development" chapter promote a culture-oriented education, whereby educators accommodate the preferred learning styles of culturally diverse students. Watson's learning, involvement, and educational gains model is again used to clarify the notion of culture in learning. Discussions about subcultures and differences—in particular how some subcultures have been historically disadvantaged and marginalized on college campuses—dominate this chapter. A more explicit discussion of some of the sociopolitical issues that are seldom explicitly discussed would have been a welcome addition.

The authors of chapters 4 to 6 apply the theories explained in the opening chapters to diverse contexts. In the "Learning and Development from Theory to Practice," chapter, Cuyjet and Lewis Newman provide familiar examples of how theory can be used to deliver high quality services and programs to students. Four key issues—facilitating the needs of new students, developing community, developing value, and instilling a service mindset— central to the student learning agenda are detailed. De la Teja and Kramer's "Student Affairs and Learning in the College Community" chapter focuses on student learning in community colleges. This example crystallizes for readers the interrelationship between context and student learning. Their analyses highlight the diverse and overlooked learning needs of diverse student populations and marginalized educational settings. In the "Service Learning: Exemplifying the Connections between Theory and Practice" chapter, Muller and Stage apply four learning theories discussed earlier in the text to service-learning programs. These discussions reinforce a reoccurring theme in the book and in student affairs— student affairs professionals should play a central role in enhancing student learning.

The assessment chapter, written by Upcraft, begins by clarifying the distinction between assessment and evaluation. Later, Upcraft offers step-by-step tips for novices desiring to measure learning quantitatively and qualitatively. The recommended procedures appear deceptively linear and problem-free. In the concluding chapter, "Setting a New Context for Student Learning," Stage and Watson revisit the contributors' main arguments and briefly speculate on a future agenda for higher education.

This book has notable strengths. The authors' arguments are clearly and efficiently presented using a practitioner discourse that is rooted in published research findings and practical work experiences. The case studies illustrate numerous "how-to-get-started" suggestions for student affairs staffs who want to work in harmony with faculty and other academic affairs staff.

There are two notable shortcomings in this text. The first has to do with the authors not always "practicing what they preach." For example, Stage and Muller introduce four theoretical perspectives, some of which are not commonly associated with the student learning imperative; these diverse perspectives are assets. Unfortunately, the presentation of these perspectives violates one of the primary themes of the book—holistic learning. As a reader, I wanted to know, for example, how Conscientization theory, rooted in liberation theology, interconnects with the multiple intelligences discussion that is rooted in cognitive science. The authors' interdisciplinary meaning making is absent, creating the perception that the choices were haphazard. This perception is reinforced when some of the primary literature linking intellectual development with student learning (e.g., see King's [1996] synthesis of research on student cognition and learning) is barely mentioned.

This absence of holistic understanding is also evident when one looks across the eight chapters. Each chapter contributes to enhancing the readers' understanding of their student learning agenda, but a sense of disconnection prevails.

For example, in the second half of the book the discussion progresses from a dialogue about community colleges, to service learning, concluding with an assessment discussion. These three topics are important and could interrelate, but the connections are seldom made. The sense of wholeness, which is a professed core value of the editors, is too often absent.

A second shortcoming centers on the editors' goal of advancing "new ways of looking at old problems" (p. 2). The literature the editors cite in the introductory chapter suggests that their student learning agenda has been around for at least thirty years. Explicitly discussing reasons why academia has been reluctant to get on the "student learning bandwagon" would have been a welcome addition to the text, especially because many of the contributors' suggestions have been previously recommended. Specifically addressing past impediments is an important prerequisite to advancing "new ways of looking at old problems."

Stage, Watson, and Terrell suggest that the intended audience is broad, including student affairs professionals, faculty, and preparatory faculty of student affairs professionals. These intended audiences would be well served by the book if they were unfamiliar with why student learning is central to the mission of student affairs, in particular, and higher education, in general, or if readers were planning a student learning initiative for the first time.

## References

King, P. M. (1996). Student cognition and learning. In S. Komives and D. B. Woodard (Eds.), *Student services: A handbook for the profession* (pp. 218–243). San Francisco: Jossey-Bass.

---

*Prioritizing Academic Programs and Services: Reallocating Resources to Achieve Strategic Balance,* by Robert C. Dickeson. Foreword by Stanley O. Ikenberry. San Francisco: Jossey-Bass, 1999. 192 pp. $34.95.

DON G. CREAMER, Virginia Polytechnic Institute and State University

Stanley Ikenberry says that there is no more difficult or more important job in higher education than clarifying purposes and setting priorities for colleges and universities. Accomplishing this task is vital because institutions do not have inexhaustible resources, and the link between academic quality and financial health of institutions is clear. Robert Dickeson offers a road map for setting and shaping these priorities.

Dickeson gained his expertise in the trenches, serving as a teacher, an academic administrator, a university president, and a private organization consultant with leaders of colleges and universities. His mission in this book is to apply what he learned from his experiences to help institutions achieve a tighter focus of academic programs and services and to make better use of their resources.

He accomplishes this purpose by providing a "step-by-step guide for confronting the many dimensions of academic program prioritization" (p. xix).

The author begins by recounting internal and external pressures for reform in higher education and states seven premises for reform. Among the premises are the centrality of academic programs to the collegiate institution, the absence of judgments of worth of an ever increasing number of academic programs, and the failure of traditional across-the-board cuts to adequately address institutional needs to reallocate resources. He also argues that adding new academic programs under current conditions results in diminution of resources for existing programs and that there is too much of what he calls "runaway specialization" in colleges and universities. Curriculum creep leads to program creep that leads to mission creep in his view. In the end, Dickeson contends that "the price for academic program bloat for all is impoverishment of each" (p. 17).

Dickeson's plan recognizes the vital requirement for leadership to accomplish program prioritization and reallocation of resources. He addresses specifically the roles of the president, the board, and the provost and points out that leadership and courage are required. He asks these leaders a series of questions as a form of "gut check" about whether the institution is prepared to undergo the process of prioritization. If they are, then Dickeson calls for a reaffirmation of the institutional mission. In this process, he seeks clarity, but he recognizes some special issues such as political considerations, accreditation, and the reality that purposes change over time. A major reason that clarity is essential to achieve consensus about mission is that "centrality to mission" is a major criterion for judging program worth in Dickeson's plan.

Defining programs is problematic, even in Dickeson's scheme, but he offers an operational definition that seems logical for his purposes. A program is "any activity or collection of activities of the institution that consumes resources" (p. 44). The requirement is to identify programs, not departments, and to identify programs in their most elemental form. It is at this basic level that the judgments about program quality and centrality must be made. For the record, Dickeson seeks to evaluate student affairs programs just as he does academic programs, but frankly, does not address this process thoroughly.

Dickeson suggests using 10 indicators, some quantitative and some qualitative, against which to judge program quality and centrality to mission:

1. History, development, and expectations of the program;
2. External demand for the program;
3. Internal demand for the program;
4. Quality of program inputs and processes;
5. Quality of program outcomes;
6. Size, scope, and productivity of the program;
7. Revenue and other resources generated by the program;
8. Costs and other expenses associated with the program;
9. Impact, justification, and overall essentiality of the program; and
10. Opportunity analysis of the program.

In keeping with his step-by-step approach, Dickeson suggests precisely what to do and what data and in what order data should be collected. He suggests scaling methods for the 10 indicators and precisely the number of points to be assigned to each. After data are collected, he calls for "levels of judgment"; that is, that departments should rank the data first, then directors or deans, vice presidents, and finally, the president. After this ranking process by levels, further ranking is suggested for all programs by categories to yield five levels of possible action. The upper 20% may be candidates for enrichment, the next 20% might be retained for higher level of support, the next 20% retained at neutral level of support, the next 20% retained at a lower level of support, and the lowest 20% become candidates for reduction, phasing out, or consolidation. In Dickeson's scheme, each category must contain exactly 20% of the institutional programs.

Dickeson anticipates questions that will be raised about the prioritization process and suggests some process remedies, then addresses decisions about enrichment or expansion of current programs and adding new programs. He confronts issues associated with reduction of programs, elimination of programs, and consolidation or restructuring of programs. He acknowledges legal and policy implications such as reduction in force (RIF) policies and tenure issues. He discusses accreditation issues and humane dimensions of making serious program changes.

In conclusion, Dickeson summarizes the external and the internal forces that affect program prioritization and suggests that they be used in a force-field analysis to help institutions achieve a "strategic balance" in teaching, research, and service; purposes; fiscal expectations; congruence; and affordability and accessibility. Strategic balance also is sought in stability and flexibility; harmonizing institutional interest and public interests; respecting tradition and readying for the future; reconciling competing expectations; integrating liberal arts and career preparation; planning top down and bottom up; and delineating authority and responsibility. An ambitious agenda indeed!

The step-by-step plan for program prioritization offered in this book may be particularly useful for college and university administrators and for members of boards of trustees. The book does not make a unique contribution, however, except in its progressive and step-by-step approach to program restructuring. Calls for reform of program priorities are common in higher education literature. David Leslie and E. K. Fretwell, Jr., in *Wise Moves in Hard Times*, for example, devote a section to searching for solutions just as Dickeson described. In *Restructuring Higher Education*, Terrence MacTaggart discusses contexts for change, case studies, and lessons learned from restructuring efforts that are driven by the same forces that Dickeson identifies. Likewise, Ami Zusman specifically includes institutional retrenchment and reallocation in a discussion of "Issues in Higher Education" (found in Philip Altbach, Robert Berdahl, and Patricia Gumport, *American Higher Education in the Twenty-first Century*).

The book has its shortcomings. It is never clear, for example, whether Dickeson is talking about all academic programs within an institution or whether he is talking only about undergraduate programs. He tries to differentiate between major institution types in his plan, but this is not accomplished very successfully, because he provides only surface distinctions and does not address the use of his plan by type of institution. His call for comprehensive reform leaves one to wonder whether his arguments for reform really suggest that department heads, deans, vice presidents, and provosts are not doing their jobs very well and that if they were, the kind of pervasive tactic Dickeson supports might not be necessary. Further, one wonders why such a extensive tactic as Dickeson advocates would not be better accomplished in concert with some other compelling need to conduct a self-study, such as during regional accreditation reaffirmation. Dickeson never explains why this approach is best conducted as a stand-alone initiative.

Overall, the book is worthwhile for institutional leaders trying to achieve tighter focus of academic programs and services. Because this is a general interest of these leaders, the book should have a widespread appeal.

*References*

Altbach, P. G., Berdahl, R. O., & Gumport, P. J. (Eds.). (1999). *American higher education in the twenty-first century: Social, political, and economic challenges.* Baltimore, MD: The Johns Hopkins University Press.

Leslie, D. W., & Fretwell, E. K., Jr. (1996). *Wise moves in hard times: Creating and managing resilient colleges and universities.* San Francisco: Jossey-Bass.

MacTaggart, T. J., & Associates. (1996). *Restructuring higher education: What works and what doesn't in reorganizing governing systems.* San Francisco: Jossey-Bass.

Zusman, A. (1999). *Issues facing higher education in the twenty-first century.* In P. G. Altbach, R. O. Berdahl, & P. J. Gumport (Eds.), *American higher education in the twenty-first century: Social, political, and economic challenges* (pp. 109–148). Baltimore, MD: The Johns Hopkins University Press.

*Shattering the Myths: Women in Academe,* by
Judith Glazer-Raymo. Baltimore, MD: The Johns
Hopkins University Press, 1999. 208+ pp. $38.00

FLORENCE A. HAMRICK, Iowa State University

In *Shattering the Myths,* the author uses feminist perspectives to analyze gender representation in higher education and the persistence of gender-related disparities. She also analyzes several prevailing assumptions and practices in which disparities are anchored that serve to hinder women's progress within higher education. These include seemingly gender-neutral practices such as faculty employment tracks, assignment of merit criteria, and specification of accountability measures. For the most part, these are the myths that Glazer-Raymo seeks to expose and, in turn, shatter through presenting evidence that "gender neutrality is a fiction in the professoriate and in academic administration" (p. 24). She then provides and discusses suggestions and recommendations for promising strategies.

In Chapter 1, "The Personal and the Professional: Becoming a Feminist," Glazer-Raymo recalls more than thirty years of her own life as an educator, administrator, and feminist in light of evolving social and political developments like Title IX, affirmative action policies, and the expansion of higher education. Major trends and issues identified in the first chapter are woven through the remainder of the book. Some readers may be impatient with the biographical technique in the first chapter, because the narrative clearly draws the author's life (Reinharz, 1992) into a scholarly examination of public policy issues and problems. However, this technique effectively reinforces the message that lives unfold against sociopolitical backdrops that shape assumptions and careers, and these backdrops and assumptions must be well understood if change is to be possible.

In Chapters 2 through 5, Glazer-Raymo examines the academic labor market; tenure, promotion, and salaries; professional women (e.g., lawyers, dentists); and women administrators. Some common problems are echoed, such as women's underrepresentation in male-dominated and higher paying disciplines, affecting not only women's prestige but bargaining power. For example, she demonstrates how women in male-dominated professions enter not a "free market" of ideas or efforts, but enter instead a complex network of inherited structures that function to advantage traditional insiders whose values and privileges the structures manifest. Glazer-Raymo discusses the subtle forms of harassment and segregation that are evidence of general reluctance toward inclusiveness, equity, and valuing women's scholarship. However, the news is not uniformly positive with respect to legal redress, based on Glazer-Raymo's summary of the mixed success with respect to individual court cases.

These middle chapters synthesize evidence from case law and legislation, employment figures, and enrollment statistics. In her final analysis, echoing Tierney and Bensimon's (1996) work, access to education—even advanced education—and entry into (academic) work are not the sites of the most intractable problems faced by women. Advancement, equitable remuneration, and valuing the contributions of people who largely remain cultural outsiders are the persistent problems. The reasons for these disparities are complex, and problem sources are not easily identified or essentialized. However, Glazer-Raymo's book excels at identifying issues, contextualizing them within social and political climates that are continually evolving and substantiating explanations for their persistence.

In the final chapters on implementing change and conclusions, Glazer-Raymo discusses two potential strategies for change—campus commissions and feminist pedagogy. Campus commissions focus attention on local evidence of disparities and, more recently, defend existing operations and programs in the current climate of feminist backlash. Several examples of effective commissions were cited. Glazer-Raymo's promotion of localized study and action through commissions as an effective strategy subsequently has been reinforced by the recent publicity surrounding documentation of gender discrimination at MIT's School of Science (Wilson, 1999) and by plans for institutional redress. Time will tell whether local commission strategies are effective for groups on other campuses who are now engaged in similar efforts. Following the MIT example, what may perhaps emerge are derivative commissions that focus not on an entire campus with its broad collection of disciplines and fields of study but instead on colleges or subsets of related disciplines with somewhat more shared notions of discrimination indicators (e.g., laboratory space among scientists). Such a trend would also be consistent with Glazer-Raymo's earlier analysis of feminism proceeding from its early emphasis on broadly-focused, collective social action to its later emergence in subgroups—albeit not always respected subgroups—within individual professional or disciplinary associations.

With respect to the second strategy of feminist pedagogy, Glazer-Raymo claims: "Engendering pedagogical theory and practice and building on knowledge gained through two decades of feminist pedagogy provides practical strategies for changing classroom and campus cultures" (p. 195). There seems little doubt that feminist pedagogy (features of which are also echoed in adult education literature) serve to enrich the learning environment for students. It is less clear that improved pedagogical practices will lead to campus cultural or organizational transformation—particularly a transformation that will benefit women academics who enlist these pedagogies. Despite more widespread calls for effective teaching (e.g., Wingspread Group, 1993) and attempts to reinterpret teaching as a form of scholarship (e.g., Boyer, 1990), there is less persuasive evidence that the research-teaching-service scaffold has been successfully toppled at individual campuses. This is especially the case for prestigious institutions where stature is clearly grounded in research and grant activity. Unfortunately, until a shift in thought and action becomes apparent, emphasizing teaching and feminist pedagogy may serve instead as reinforcement of the notion of women performing the women's work of academe (Park, 1996).

In summary, *Shattering the Myths* is an extremely important book. Glazer-Raymo highlights evolving social, political, and institutional forces surrounding gender issues and women's representation as well as the myths shaping perceptions of gender equity in academe. She clearly documents evidence of persistent disparities; reveals multiple, reinforcing sources of discrimination; and offers strategies to address discrimination. Perhaps most importantly, Glazer-Raymo demonstrates that although gender discrimination has evolved and now appears in different forms, it nonetheless remains a characteristic feature of academe, and women academics continue to pay a disproportionate price.

## References

Boyer, E. L. (1990). *Scholarship reconsidered: Priorities of the professoriate.* Lawrenceville, NJ: Princeton University Press.

Park, S. M. (1996). Research, teaching, and service: Why shouldn't women's work count? *Journal of Higher Education, 67,* 46–84.

Reinharz, S. (1992). *Feminist methods in social research.* New York: Oxford University Press.

Tierney, W. G., & Bensimon, E. M. (1996). *Promotion and tenure: Community and socialization in academe.* Albany, NY: State University of New York Press.

Wilson, R. (1999). An MIT professor's suspicion of bias leads to a new movement for academic women. *Chronicle of Higher Education, 46*(15), pp. A16–A18.

Wingspread Group on Higher Education. (1993). *An American imperative: Higher expectations for higher education.* Racine, WI: Johnson Foundation.

# Instructions to Contributors

Manuscripts should be mailed in triplicate to Leonard L. Baird, Editor, *The Journal of Higher Education,* Ohio State University Press, 1070 Carmack Road, Columbus, OH 43210-1002.

**Style.** *The Journal of Higher Education* has adopted as its official guide the *Publication Manual of the American Psychological Association,* fourth edition, and all manuscripts should be brought into conformity with this guide before they are submitted. Papers should be typed, double-spaced, on white $8^1/2 \times 11$-inch paper, with wide margins. Upon acceptance, contributors will be asked to supply a computer file on an IBM-compatible standard disk in WordPerfect. Authors who use a different system should prepare an ASCII text file. An abstract of fifty words or less, summarizing the main points of the article, should accompany the manuscript. Because the journal's readers represent a variety of professional interests, it is recommended that any statistical material be presented as briefly and simply as possible. Although each paper submitted should deal with the methodology employed in addressing the subject in sufficient detail to place the data within the proper methodological setting, the editors of the journal are not primarily interested in papers setting forth practices of research methods (an acquaintance with fundamental procedures of scholarly analysis being assumed on the part of the reader) except for those papers that develop innovative methodological approaches.

Illustrations submitted with the final draft must be of professional quality, and executed on white paper or vellum, in black ink, with clear, medium weight, black lines and figures. Typewritten lettering should not appear in illustrations. Figures should be provided **at size**—no larger than $4^1/2 \times 7$ inches (full page) and preferably no larger that $4^1/2 \times 3^1/2$ inches (half page) and **printed camera-ready at a minimum of 600 dpi.** They should be numbered consecutively, and the number and author's name should be penciled lightly on the back of each. All illustrations must have captions, which should not appear on the artwork but should be typed, double-spaced, on a sheet at the end of the manuscript. If there is any potential for doubt, the word *top* should be written on the back of the illustration.

Authors should employ a Reference List format to list bibliographic data. Endnotes should be reserved for supplementary comment and typed on a separate page at the end of the manuscript.

**Manuscript Length.** Manuscripts averaging 25–30 pages of double-spaced typescript are preferred, but the editors will consider longer papers on topics requiring a fuller treatment.

**Review Process.** Those unsolicited manuscripts that are refereed are reviewed blind. Authors are thus requested to submit their name, professional position, and institution on a removable cover sheet. They should also mask any items of self-reference where they appear. Authors must not submit the manuscript of any article that is still under consideration by another publisher.

**Editorial Reaction.** Papers will not be returned to authors if they fail to meet by a wide margin the basic criteria for selection. Otherwise, authors may expect to receive some notification within three months. If an article is accepted, it will usually appear in print within twelve months after acceptance. If an article that has been subjected to a full review is rejected, the opinions of the referees will be transmitted to the author.

**Criteria for Selection.** Papers are evaluated on the following points: Form: writing style and readability, logical development, appropriate length, appropriateness of author's stated objectives to treatment as defined below. Content: significance to *JHE* readers. Additional criteria are based upon the following manuscript orientations: as a research paper, as a technical paper, as a professional practice paper, as a literature review, and as a policy paper. It should be emphasized that the editors respond most favorably to manuscripts that evidence both a freshness of vision and a vitality that may be informed by, but certainly go beyond, methodological qualities, and that are in congruence with our publishing goals and directions. The most effective approach in learning about our interests is to read previous issues of the journal. We expect that authors, the journal, and the field will develop through the publication process.

# Administrative Science Quarterly

*Dedicated to advancing the understanding of administration through empirical investigation and theoretical analysis.*

http://www.johnson.cornell.edu/ASQ/asq.html

**Upcoming in *ASQ*:**

"Institutional Sources of Practice Variation: Staffing College and University Recycling Programs"
**Michael Lounsbury**

"Contours of Organizational Improvisation and Learning"
**Anne S. Miner, Paula Bassoff, and Christine Moorman**

"Cultural Diversity at Work: The Moderating Effects of Work Group Perspectives on Diversity"
**Robin J. Ely and David A. Thomas**

"Well-Networked Challengers, Established Elites, and Owning Families: A Social Class Theory of the Diversifying Acquisitions of Large U.S. Corporations in the 1960s"
**Donald Palmer and Brad N. Barber**

"Institutions, Exchange Relations, and the Emergence of New Fields: Regulatory Policies and Independent Power Production in Amercian, 1978-1992"
**Michael V. Russo**

**Special Issue: June 1998:** Critical Perspectives on Organizational Control
**Stephen R. Barley and John M. Jermier, eds.**

**ADMINISTRATIVE SCIENCE QUARTERLY**

Cornell University, 20 Thornwood Dr., Suite 100
Ithaca, NY 14850-1265   (607) 254-7143

Published quarterly:   March, June, September, and December
by the Johnson Graduate School of Management
**Back issues, 1982–1992, $6.00 each or 1993-Present, $15.00 each**

Begin a subscription with    ☐ current issue    ☐ the _____ issue

Individual ☐ $65.00    Student (with proof of I.D.) ☐ $30.00    Institution ☐ $130.00
**U.S. dollars only**
Additional postage (per year) outside the U.S.                    $10.00 ☐    Airmail, $40.00 ☐

☐ Visa    ☐ Mastercard   No. _____        Expiration date_____

☐ Payment enclosed    ☐ Bill me   Signature _____

Name_____

Address_____

City_____ State_____ Zip_____

Rates subject to change.                                                            12/00

# The Journal of Higher Education

*Published bimonthly*

---

*If you would like to subscribe, please complete and return this form.*

Subscription Rates, Volume 72, 2001:
Individual: $42.00  Student: $28.00  Institution: $90.00   Foreign postage: $7.00
Association Member: $28.00 (Circle one)  AAHE  ACPA  AIR  ASHE  NADE  NASPA

Please enter my/our subscription to *The Journal of Higher Education,* Vol. 72, 2001.

❏ I / We enclose a check/money order made payable to Ohio State University.

(Canadian residents, please add 7% GST. Our GST number is 123995904. All orders must be prepaid by credit card, check, or money order. Only individual orders may be paid with personal check.)

Please charge my            ❏ MasterCard            ❏ Visa

Account Number _____  Exp. date _____

Signature _____ Date _____

*Please print*

Name _____

Address _____

City _____  State/Province _____ Zip Code _____

Phone Number _____  E-mail Address _____

Journals are mailed second class USPS in North America and to the rest of the world. Allow four to six weeks for delivery. No refunds of subscriptions will be made after the first issue of the journal for the year has been mailed. Prices subject to change without notice.

---

**Please return this form to:**
Journal Subscriptions Manager
Ohio State University Press, 1070 Carmack Road, Columbus, OH 43210-1002, USA

OHIO
STATE

E-mail: ohiostatepress@osu.edu
or Call 614-292-1407